Generational Shift

*Shift Mindsets, Break Cycles, and
Embrace New Ideas for Africa's Growth*

By Kenety Sonsanah Gee

Copyright © 2025 by Kenety Sonsanah Gee
All rights reserved.

No part of this publication may be reproduced, stored in a retrieval system, or transmitted in any form or by any means — electronic, mechanical, photocopying, recording, or otherwise — without the prior written permission of the publisher, except in the case of brief quotations used in reviews or scholarly work.

Generational Shift: Shift Mindsets, Break Cycles, and Embrace New Ideas for Africa's Growth
ISBN: 978-1-968098-08-7

First Edition
Published by AllState Publishers
www.allstatepublishers.com

Printed in the United States of America

This is a work of nonfiction. Any similarities to actual people, organizations, or events are purely coincidental unless specifically stated.

For permissions, inquiries, or speaking engagements, please contact: connect@kenetygee.com

A roadmap for Africa's true independence. At a very crucial moment when Africa stands at a crossroads, *Generational Shift* provides a clear roadmap for self-reliance, innovation, and sustainable development. With critical analysis and unwavering optimism, Kenety Gee paints a clear portrait of Africa's limitless potential and enviable destiny when its people embrace a new paradigm shift of thinking beyond old limitations and embrace bold, transformative ideas.

Bishop Nathanial N. Zarway, Sr.

Diocesan Bishop, Church of our Lord Jesus Christ of the Apostolic Faith Inc. West Africa and Senior Pastor – Greater Refuge Cathedral

Monrovia, Liberia

As a member of the African diaspora, *Generational Shift* resonates deeply with me. Kenety S. Gee challenges us to break free from inherited cycles and actively shape Africa's future with bold vision and innovation. This book is a call to action – one that urges us to invest in Africa's potential, redefine success on our terms, and build a sustainable, prosperous future for generations to come. A must-read for anyone committed to Africa's transformation.

G. Lan Ijiwola, Ph.D.

CEO, Life Development Center Chicago, Illinois, USA

Against pessimism that has at times plagued minds regarding the future of Africa because of the continent's many challenges, Kenety Gee's book strikes a note of optimism rooted, not in illusions of progress, but in concrete actions that several African nations have undertaken to lift themselves out of poverty and prosper. This movement toward development attests to a change in the mindset of the new generation in Africa and ushers both the continent and the rest of the world to the African Dream. I highly recommend this book to everyone interested in learning about Africa as it was, is, and will be.

Rev. Dr. Stéphane M. Kalonji

Adjunct Professor of Humanities and Philosophy Wharton County Junior College, Texas, USA

A Call to Action for Africa's Growth

Generational Shift is more than just a book – it is a movement. With a bold and refreshing perspective, Kenety Gee challenges outdated mindsets that have held Africa back for generations. This book is a call to action for Africans to embrace new ideas, break destructive cycles, and chart a future of true independence and prosperity.

Chipiliro L. Kansilanga

Media and Communications – African Union Arusha, Tanzania

I highly recommend this book to anyone seeking a deeper understanding of the complexities and opportunities facing Africa today. Kenety Gee's work is a significant contribution to the ongoing conversation about Africa's future, and it is a must-read for anyone committed to the continent's progress and prosperity. If you are passionate about progress, social justice, and unlocking Africa's vast potential, this book will inspire and challenge you in equal measure.

Dr. Harry Papa Mason
Adjunct Professor of Business
Dunwoody College of Technology, Minnesota, USA

To my beloved wife, Naipaye Jaiway Gee, my Rose of Sharon, my beautiful dove.

Thank you for your patience, your unwavering support, words of encouragement, and giving me the space and time to bring this project to life. Your love and understanding have been my greatest strength on this journey.

Acknowledgments

The journey of writing this book has been one of deep reflection, rigorous inquiry, and unwavering commitment to the future of Africa. However, no great work is ever accomplished in isolation. Many individuals have played a vital role in bringing this book to life, and I am profoundly grateful for their support, encouragement, and contributions.

First, I am deeply grateful to my wife, Naipaye Jaiway Gee, and family, friends, and mentors who have walked with me on this journey. Your unwavering support and belief in this vision have given me the strength to push forward, even in moments of doubt. Your encouragement has been a source of inspiration, reminding me that this work is not just about words on a page but about shaping a future that we can all be proud of.

I extend my heartfelt appreciation to Mattie Murrey-Tegels for her keen editorial eye, insightful feedback, and invaluable guidance throughout the writing process. Her meticulous attention to detail, thoughtful suggestions, and steadfast dedication to clarity and coherence have greatly enhanced the depth and readability of this work. Her expertise has been a guiding light, ensuring that my message is communicated with precision and impact.

To the countless thinkers, scholars, and changemakers – past and present – who have inspired the ideas in this book, I acknowledge your influence. Your work and dedication to Africa's progress have laid the foundation upon which we build today.

Lastly, to this generation of Africans who dare to think differently, challenge the status quo, and embrace the promise of a brighter future – this book is for you. May it serve as a beacon of hope, a call to action, and a reminder that the power to shape Africa's destiny lies in our hands.

With gratitude,

Kenety S. Gee

Foreword

Africa, the continent of my birth and my passion, is at a pivotal moment in its history. From Monrovia to Nairobi, from Lagos to Addis Ababa, the pulse of change beats ever louder. Yet, despite our vast potential and abundant resources, we continue to struggle with many of the same challenges that have plagued us for generations – structural economic weaknesses, capital flight, brain drain, governance failures, and social divisions.

As someone who has had the privilege of serving in government, international finance, and development, I have seen firsthand both the promise of Africa and the roadblocks that hinder its rise. We have no shortage of talent. Our youth are among the most innovative and ambitious in the world. Our diaspora communities excel in every sector, from technology to medicine, from entrepreneurship to academia. And yet, too often, we find ourselves trapped in old ways of thinking

– ways that have not yielded the progress our people deserve.

That is why *Generational Shift: Shift Mindsets, Break Cycles, and Embrace New Ideas for Africa's Growth* is such a timely and important contribution. This book does not merely diagnose Africa's problems; it presents a vision for a new way forward. It challenges us to rethink the policies, mindsets, and habits that have kept Africa from reaching its full potential. More importantly, it urges us to embrace bold, transformative ideas that will unlock the true power of the continent.

At the heart of this book is a call for a new economic and social philosophy – one that moves us beyond dependency and toward sustainable, homegrown solutions. We cannot afford to remain mere participants in a global economic system that does not always serve our best interests.

Instead, we must become architects of our own destiny, strengthening our institutions, fostering intra-African trade, investing in education and innovation, and creating an Africa where prosperity is not the privilege of a few but the right of all.

The chapter on "Opportunity Economies for Greater Human Flourishing" particularly resonates with me. Having worked in finance and development, I have long argued that economic growth, when properly managed, must translate into real and tangible improvements in people's lives. A strong economy is not just about GDP figures or foreign direct investment; it is about whether young Africans can find decent jobs, whether families can live in dignity, and whether our policies empower the next generation to dream bigger than the last.

Equally important is the book's emphasis on the role of the diaspora in Africa's development. Many of our finest minds have found themselves outside the continent, contributing immensely to economies elsewhere.

But what if we could create an environment that welcomes their expertise back home? What if Africa's brain drain could be turned into a brain gain? The book makes a compelling case for how we can harness the strength of our global African family for the benefit of our nations.

The message is clear: Africa's future is not a question of fate; it is a matter of choice. The future we want will not be handed to us – it must be built through visionary leadership, collective effort, and a willingness to break with the past where necessary. Change is not easy, but as history shows, it is those who dare to think differently who shape the world.

I commend Kenety S. Gee for this insightful and courageous work. This book is not just a collection of ideas; it is a roadmap for those who believe in an Africa that is self-sufficient, confident, and prosperous.

It is an urgent call to action, not just for governments and policymakers, but for every African – on the continent and beyond – who dares to believe in a brighter tomorrow.

The next chapter of Africa's story is ours to write. May we write it boldly and confidently.

Augustine Kpehe Ngafuan

Minister of Finance and Development Planning, Republic of Liberia Former Country Manager for Uganda, African Development Bank

Preface

Africa stands at a defining moment in its history. Across the continent, we are confronted by the realities of both profound challenges and boundless opportunities. As the world rapidly evolves, Africa's response must be equally dynamic—driven not by the echoes of outdated mindsets, but by a bold embrace of new ideas that reflect our current realities and future aspirations.

Generational Shift: Shift Mindsets, Break Cycles, and Embrace New Ideas for Africa's Growth is a passion project, born out of a deep desire to see Africa flourish—not just in potential, but in reality. This book reflects on the historical patterns and inherited mindsets that have constrained progress for generations. At its heart is a call to action for a new generation—one willing to question, challenge, and ultimately break free from the cycles that have held Africans back.

The journey of writing this book has been fueled by a love for Africa and a hope that its people—

both at home and in the diaspora—can come together to envision and enact a future of true independence, prosperity, and inclusion. It explores critical issues such as brain drain, capital flight, trade deficits, social justice, and the power of aspirational thinking, while also offering pathways and principles that can guide us toward an Africa where every individual has the opportunity to thrive.

This book is not just a reflection on the present; it is a bridge to the future. Each chapter serves as a beacon—an invitation to explore, rethink, and reimagine. We must move beyond external dependencies and outdated loyalties and embrace a vision that fosters self-reliance, innovation, and interconnectedness within the global community.

To the reader—whether you are a young African seeking a way forward, a leader faced with difficult choices, a member of the diaspora yearning to contribute, or simply someone who believes in Africa's promise—this book is for you. My hope is that it ignites conversation, encourages action, and inspires a lasting commitment to a brighter, bolder, and more inclusive Africa.

Together, let us break the cycles of the past and build the Africa of our dreams.

Introduction   1

Chapter 1 Reimagining Tradition: Navigating the Old and the New   5

Chapter 2: The Power of Innovation: Unleashing Africa's Potential   14

Chapter 3: Education for a New Era: Building Future Leaders   26

Chapter 4: Governance and Accountability: Redefining Leadership in Africa   37

Chapter 5: Entrepreneurship and Economic Freedom: Creating a Path to Prosperity   50

Chapter 6: Righteousness and Justice: The Call for Moral and Just Leadership   65

Chapter 7: Social Justice and Inclusion: Bridging the Gaps   71

Chapter 8: African Youth as Catalysts – Empowering the Next Generation for Change   88

Chapter 9: Capital Escape – Curbing Financial Flight from African Economies   97

Chapter 10: Building a Culture of Innovation and Entrepreneurship   110

Chapter 11: Women as Pioneers of Change in African Societies — 130

Chapter 12: Environmental Stewardship and Sustainable Development — 142

Chapter 13: The Effects of Trade Deficits on the African Economy — 158

Chapter 14: Opportunity Economies for Greater Human Flourishing — 164

Chapter 15: From Poverty Alleviation to Prosperity: Shifting the Focus to Wealth Creation — 169

Chapter 16: Africa's New Fight: From Dependency to Global Leadership — 181

Chapter 17: The Role of Africa's Diaspora in Advancing Progress — 195

Chapter 18: Chasing the African Dream — 208

Chapter 19: A Vision for Africa's Future – Pathways to True Independence and Prosperity — 215

References — 227

Introduction

Africa stands at a pivotal crossroads. It is a continent rich in history, culture, and potential—home to some of the brightest and most creative minds in the world. For generations, its children have navigated a complex landscape shaped by deeply ingrained ideas and rigid mindsets. While these traditional ways of thinking have provided stability and continuity in times of adversity, they have also become barriers to progress in an increasingly modern and globalized world.

As we move further into the 21st century, it is clear that the challenges and opportunities facing Africa demand more than resilience—they require innovation, adaptability, and a willingness to embrace change. You are called to this task: to innovate, to adapt, and to embrace a shift in mindset and transformation.

Generational Shift: Shift Mindsets, Break Cycles, and Embrace New Ideas for Africa's Growth is a call to action for a new era of thought and leadership.

Introduction

This book argues that the time has come to reassess the ideas and mindsets that have long governed our families and societies. While we must honor and preserve the traditions that ground us, we must also be willing to question them, to innovate, and to develop new ways of thinking that meet the demands of today's world.

The transformation we seek is ultimately a shift in perspective. The old ways, while once valuable, may no longer serve a continent striving for growth, equality, and sustainability.

The new wine of fresh ideas and forward-thinking solutions cannot be poured into the old wineskins of outdated practices.

> "The new wine of fresh ideas and forward- thinking solutions cannot be poured into the old wineskins of outdated practices."

This transformation must begin now—with today's generation of Africans ready to challenge the status quo, break free from cycles of dependency and stagnation, and lead the way toward a future that reflects the continent's true potential. Are you ready to answer the call?

Africa must wean itself from cycles of dependency—and that process begins with you, your family, and your community. We are long past the era of colonization; the time is ripe for Africa to rise to its latent heights. This book posits that a shift in generational mindsets is necessary to launch a new trajectory for Africa's growth. It starts with you. You are the change needed for this continental new dawn—one that ushers in thriving, equitable societies at every level.

In this book, we will explore the areas where generational shift is most needed—from governance and education to entrepreneurship and social justice. We will examine how new ideas can revitalize our economies, empower our people, and build societies that are not only resilient, but dynamic and inclusive.

By breaking the cycle of inherited mindsets and embracing the possibilities of the future, Africa can

Introduction

chart a course toward a more prosperous and equitable tomorrow.

Generational Shift is more than a title—it is a vision of what Africa can become when we dare to think differently, act boldly, and believe in the power of our own ideas. The journey ahead will not be easy, but it is a journey worth taking. It is the path to true liberation and lasting progress for you—and for all Africans.

Chapter 1
Reimagining Tradition: Navigating the Old and the New

Introduction

Throughout history, tradition has served as the bedrock of societies, offering continuity and identity. In Africa, these traditions have shaped communities and influenced everything from governance and social structures to education and economics. However, as the continent confronts new challenges and opportunities in an increasingly interconnected world, there is growing recognition that tradition alone may not be enough to propel Africa forward. The key lies in reimagining tradition—not abandoning it, but allowing it to evolve in ways that meet the needs of a new generation.

This chapter explores the delicate balance between preserving cultural heritage and embracing innovation. It examines how other

Chapter 1

developing nations have successfully navigated this balance, blending traditional values with modern solutions to drive generational shift. Africa can draw inspiration from these examples to craft its own path—one that honors the wisdom of the past while embracing the demands of the future.

African culture remains the cornerstone of African identity, and its enduring wisdom reminds us that adaptation is part of survival. To grow, we must not discard this identity, but we must reshape how it functions in today's context.

The Role of Tradition in African Societies

Tradition in African societies is deeply rooted in communal values, respect for elders, and adherence to cultural norms. These elements have provided a strong foundation for social cohesion and have long helped maintain peace and order within communities. However, in many cases, these same traditions can also reinforce systems that resist change, restrict opportunity, and hinder progress.

For instance, traditional governance structures—while valuable in maintaining order—can at times conflict with democratic principles. Likewise, customary practices related to gender roles and inheritance may limit the potential of women and younger generations to contribute fully to society. Addressing these challenges requires a rethinking of how tradition can be reinterpreted to support, rather than hinder, Africa's development.

Global Examples of Reimagined Traditions

Several developing nations have successfully reimagined their traditions to foster generational shifts, striking a balance between cultural preservation and modernization. These examples offer valuable insights:

Chapter 1

1. Rwanda – Reconciliation and Development through Gacaca

Rwanda's post-genocide recovery is a powerful example of how traditional structures can be reimagined to serve national healing and development. After the 1994 genocide, Rwanda reintroduced the Gacaca courts—a community-based justice system rooted in traditional restorative practices—to process a massive backlog of genocide-related cases.

These courts allowed communities to address crimes locally, often emphasizing confession, repentance, and reconciliation. By adapting this traditional model within a modern legal framework, Rwanda fostered healing while maintaining cultural relevance. Today, Rwanda is recognized for its strong governance, gender equity, and economic growth—all rooted in a thoughtful blend of tradition and innovation.

2. South Korea – The New Village Movement (Saemaul Undong)

In the 1970s, South Korea launched the Saemaul Undong or "New Village Movement" to modernize rural areas while preserving communal values. Emphasizing self-help, diligence, and cooperation, the movement transformed rural economies and laid the groundwork for South Korea's industrial rise. Its success came from merging traditional values with modern goals—a powerful lesson in how tradition can evolve without losing its essence.

3. Bhutan – Gross National Happiness

Bhutan's national philosophy prioritizes Gross National Happiness (GNH) over Gross Domestic Product (GDP), grounded in Buddhist traditions that emphasize communal well-being and harmony with nature. By embedding these spiritual values into government policy, Bhutan created a development model that emphasizes sustainability, mental health, and social cohesion—demonstrating how tradition can

Chapter 1

inform modern governance in a deeply relevant way.

Applying Lessons to Africa

The challenge for Africa—and for each of its nations—is to identify aspects of tradition that can be reimagined in service of growth and equity. This process begins at the community level, where families must be willing to critically assess existing practices and engage in open dialogue about their relevance today.

Openness to innovation is essential, particularly in areas such as governance, education, and social justice. The question is not whether tradition should be preserved, but how it can be redefined to support a thriving, modern Africa.

Governance

Reshaping traditional governance structures to align with democratic principles is crucial for Africa's political stability and growth. This may involve integrating traditional councils with formal government institutions, ensuring that all voices—including those of women and youth—are meaningfully represented in decision-making. By doing so, African societies can develop governance systems that are both inclusive and reflective of their cultural heritage.

> "Reimagining tradition is not about discarding the past; it is about adapting it to the realities of the present and the possibilities of the future."

Education

Africa's educational systems must evolve to blend traditional knowledge with modern skills. This can be achieved by developing curricula that honor cultural histories while preparing students

Chapter 1

for the global workforce. For instance, integrating indigenous knowledge systems with science and technology education can foster a more holistic and relevant learning experience for African youth.

Technology also offers context-specific solutions. Consider how Facebook began as Facemash, a tool to connect Harvard students—it addressed a local need before growing into a global platform. Similarly, Africa can harness technology to meet local challenges while adapting it for broader impact.

Social Justice

Addressing social inequalities rooted in traditional practices is another area where reimagining is essential. This includes challenging customs that limit the rights and opportunities of women and marginalized communities. Countries like Rwanda have demonstrated how cultural reform can promote gender equality. By drawing from such examples, African nations can reinterpret traditions in ways that advance inclusivity and justice.

Conclusion

Reimagining tradition does not mean discarding the past; it means adapting it to meet the realities of today and the potential of tomorrow. By learning from other developing nations that have successfully balanced heritage with progress, Africa can chart a path forward—one that honors its cultural roots while embracing innovation.

This generational shift is vital for building a future where all Africans can thrive, empowered by both ancestral wisdom and modern ingenuity. As this book continues, we'll explore specific areas where this reimagining is most needed, and how fresh ideas can serve as catalysts for a flourishing Africa.

Chapter 2:
The Power of Innovation: Unleashing Africa's Potential

Introduction

Africa is often referred to as the "continent of potential"—a vast and diverse land rich in natural resources, cultural heritage, and human capital. Yet despite this abundance, much of its potential remains untapped or underutilized. This chapter explores how innovation—particularly localized innovation, whether adapted from global ideas or born entirely within the African context—can unlock that potential and transform Africa into a global hub of creativity, technology, and economic growth.

Innovation in Africa is not simply about adopting the latest technologies; it's about creating solutions to long-standing challenges, adapting existing tools to local contexts, and fostering an ecosystem where creativity and entrepreneurship thrive. Its real power lies in its ability to transcend traditional barriers and generate opportunity where none existed before.

> "Unlike imported solutions that are often costly to obtain or fail to address specific local needs, localized innovation emerges from within the community, drawing upon indigenous knowledge, resources, and insights."

Creating opportunity is one of Africa's greatest imperatives. Across the continent, people—especially the youth—are searching for better futures. Too often, this search points outward, toward opportunities in Europe, Asia, and the Americas. But the solutions may lie closer to home. This chapter highlights the untapped potential within Africa and presents practical examples of how innovation is already beginning to reshape communities, economies, and futures across the continent.

Chapter 2

Localized Innovation for the African Context

Localized innovation is essential to Africa's sustainable development. It focuses on solutions that are culturally relevant, resource-efficient, and tailored to the unique challenges of African communities. Unlike imported solutions—often costly or poorly suited to local needs—localized innovations emerge from within, drawing upon indigenous knowledge and leveraging homegrown ingenuity.

One powerful example is the success of mobile banking platforms like M-Pesa in East Africa. These services have revolutionized financial inclusion by enabling millions without access to traditional banks to save, invest, and transact—all via mobile phones. Designed with the limitations of infrastructure in mind, M-Pesa and similar platforms have created financial pathways where conventional banking systems failed to reach.

Generational Shift

In agriculture, localized innovation has enabled smallholder farmers to overcome climate and resource challenges unique to African regions. In Nigeria, Hello Tractor introduced a tractor-sharing platform that lets farmers rent machinery as needed. This eliminates the barrier of high equipment costs while improving farm productivity and income. Similarly, the development and use of drought-resistant seeds, tailored to local environmental shifts, have helped farmers withstand climate unpredictability and maintain food security.

In the healthcare sector, localized innovation is saving lives by addressing systemic limitations. In Rwanda, for instance, drones are used to deliver vital medical supplies to remote communities. Companies like Zipline work in partnership with local health authorities to overcome transportation bottlenecks and ensure rapid, reliable access to blood, vaccines, and other essentials. These are not just technological solutions—they're lifelines created in response to real, local needs.

Chapter 2

These examples underscore a growing innovation culture that values community-driven problem-solving and emphasizes sustainable, long-term impact. By fostering environments where localized innovation is encouraged, Africa can build resilient systems rooted in both tradition and forward-thinking solutions.

Africa's Untapped Potential

Africa's potential spans a wide range of sectors—from agriculture and energy to education and technology. However, persistent barriers like inadequate infrastructure, limited access to capital, and underinvestment in research and development continue to constrain this potential. Yet, every challenge presents an opportunity for innovation.

1. Agriculture: The Breadbasket of the Future

Africa holds over 60% of the world's uncultivated arable land—yet remains a net importer of food. This paradox is fueled by outdated farming methods, limited infrastructure, and inefficient market access. But innovative agricultural practices are steadily changing that reality.

Digital farming platforms in Kenya—such as M-Farm and Twiga Foods—are connecting farmers directly to markets, providing real-time pricing data, and facilitating access to quality inputs. These solutions empower smallholder farmers, boost productivity, and reduce post-harvest losses.

There is also a growing need for innovations in food storage, processing, and value addition—such as converting produce into infant food or animal feed. Addressing these gaps can dramatically reduce waste and increase economic output.

Programs like Precision Agriculture for Development (PAD) use data and mobile technology to deliver personalized farming advice. This enables farmers to make smarter decisions, increase yields, and manage their resources more sustainably.

Chapter 2

Practical Example: Off-Grid Solar Solutions

Companies like M-KOPA in East Africa are pioneering pay-as-you-go solar systems that bring affordable, clean energy to off-grid communities. These systems reduce reliance on polluting kerosene lamps while creating new opportunities—enabling small businesses to stay open longer and students to study at night.

Large-scale projects, such as Morocco's Noor Ouarzazate Solar Complex—the world's largest concentrated solar power plant—demonstrate Africa's potential to lead in sustainable energy. However, affordability remains a challenge. High unemployment and limited access to capital continue to hinder the widespread adoption of solar energy. Innovative financing and grassroots entrepreneurship are needed to make these technologies more accessible and to spur job creation.

2. Technology: The New Frontier

Africa's growing tech sector—often called the "Silicon Savannah"—is a promising engine of growth. A youthful population, widespread mobile phone use, and increasing internet connectivity are positioning the continent to become a global leader in digital innovation.

Practical Example: Fintech Revolution

Platforms like M-Pesa have reshaped financial services by enabling cashless transactions for millions without bank accounts. The model—where users convert cash into digital credit at kiosks—has sparked a wave of fintech innovation across Africa, including blockchain-based systems and mobile micro-lending platforms. These tools are not only fostering financial inclusion but also helping entrepreneurs access capital and scale their ventures.

3. Education: Cultivating Human Capital

Education is the foundation of innovation. Yet, across Africa, access to quality education is uneven, and many youth lack the skills needed for a modern workforce. Innovations in EdTech and vocational training are critical for unlocking Africa's human capital.

Chapter 2

Practical Example: EdTech Solutions

Andela, based in Nigeria, identifies and trains promising software developers, connecting them with global companies. This model provides access to high-quality education and remote job opportunities. Meanwhile, Tanzania's Ubongo uses animated multimedia to deliver educational content to children across Africa—even in remote regions. These platforms are closing the educational gap and preparing a generation of Africans to thrive in a digital economy.

Leveraging Innovation for Economic Transformation

When effectively harnessed, innovation can be a powerful catalyst for economic transformation. By focusing on high-potential sectors, Africa can build industries, generate jobs, and drive sustainable growth. But for innovation to flourish, several critical elements must be in place:

1. Investment in Research and Development (R&D)

Governments and the private sector must invest in R&D to support scientific research, technological advancement, and startup incubation. Countries like **South Korea** and **Singapore** have shown how strategic R&D investment can fuel economic prosperity.

2. A Supportive Policy Environment

Clear, innovation-friendly policies are essential. Governments must create regulatory frameworks that promote entrepreneurship, protect intellectual property, and support fair competition. Infrastructure—particularly in energy and digital access—must also be prioritized.

3. Access to Capital

Lack of financing remains a major barrier. Venture capital, impact investing, and microfinance can support startups and scale new ideas. Public-private partnerships and ethical investor negotiations are key. African leaders must advocate for the public good—not personal gain—when securing funding, resisting the temptation of kickbacks and short-term deals that undermine long-term progress.

4. Building Innovation Ecosystems

Strong ecosystems—networks of businesses, research institutions, and government bodies—foster innovation. Africa's tech hubs in Nairobi, Lagos, and Cape Town are already emerging as models, but more support is needed to strengthen these ecosystems and replicate them across the continent.

Conclusion

Africa's future lies in its ability to innovate. The continent is already home to transformative solutions—from digital farming in Kenya and solar energy in East Africa to fintech breakthroughs and educational platforms.

To unleash this potential fully, Africa must invest in research, build strong policy frameworks, increase access to capital, and nurture innovation ecosystems. Innovation is the engine that will drive Africa forward—not just to catch up, but to lead.

As we continue this journey through the book, we will explore how education, governance, and entrepreneurship can further accelerate this transformation, paving the way for a flourishing and prosperous Africa—built by its people, for its people.

Chapter 3:
Education for a New Era: Building Future Leaders

Introduction

Education is the foundation of any society's progress, and nowhere is this truer than in Africa, where a growing youth population holds immense potential to shape the continent's future. Yet to fully harness this potential, Africa must rethink its approach to education. The existing systems, often rooted in colonial-era models, are not equipped to meet the demands of the 21st century. The challenges range from outdated curricula to inadequate infrastructure and a lack of resources. However, they also present an opportunity: the chance to reform education that produces future leaders capable of driving Africa's development.

This chapter explores how Africa can revolutionize its education systems to prepare a new generation of innovators, entrepreneurs, and leaders. Drawing inspiration from successful educational models both from within Africa and from other parts of the world, it outlines how an investment in education today will yield vast future dividends.

Africa's Current Education Landscape

The education landscape in Africa is diverse, with some countries making significant progress while others continue to face deep-rooted challenges. Access to education has improved over the last two decades, particularly in primary education, but secondary and tertiary education remain underdeveloped in many regions. According to UNESCO, sub-Saharan Africa has the highest out-of-school rates for primary and secondary school-aged children. In addition, the quality of education often suffers due to large class sizes, poorly trained teachers, and a lack of learning materials. This is true both in urban and rural settings.

While these issues are prevalent, there are also pockets of success that offer valuable lessons for the continent at large. Countries like Rwanda, South Africa, and Kenya are making strides in

Chapter 3

reforming their education systems, and their experiences can guide broader reforms across the continent.

Rwanda: A Model of Reform and Innovation

Rwanda's education system is a standout example of how visionary leadership and reform can transform a country's educational landscape. In the aftermath of its 1994 genocide, Rwanda invested heavily in education as a key part of its national rebuilding strategy. The country made basic education free and compulsory and has seen enrollment in primary and secondary education soar.

Rwanda has also embraced technology as a critical component of its educational reform. The One Laptop Per Child initiative, launched in 2008, aimed to provide every primary school student with access to technology. This bold step reflects the government's recognition that digital literacy is crucial for the next generation of Rwandans to thrive in a globalized economy. Furthermore, the establishment of the Carnegie Mellon University Africa campus in Kigali has strengthened Rwanda's capacity to train future leaders in technology and engineering, with a focus on innovation and entrepreneurship.

Rwanda's example illustrates the power of national commitment and forward-thinking policies in building an education system that not only serves today's needs but also anticipates the skills and knowledge required in the future.

Kenya: A Leader in EdTech Solutions

Kenya has emerged as one of Africa's leaders in leveraging technology to improve education. Its strong innovation ecosystem has given rise to several EdTech startups that are changing the way students learn. For example, Eneza Education is an EdTech platform that provides students with access to educational content via SMS, making it particularly accessible in rural areas where internet connectivity may be limited. Eneza's platform is designed to reinforce classroom learning by offering quizzes and study materials aligned with the national curriculum.

Kenya's approach to integrating technology in education has helped bridge the gap between urban and rural students, providing more equitable access to quality learning resources. The success of EdTech solutions in Kenya highlights how innovation can overcome structural challenges in traditional education systems.

South Africa: Nurturing Future Leaders through Education

South Africa's African Leadership Academy (ALA), founded in 2008, is another shining example of how education can be designed to cultivate future leaders. ALA is a prestigious secondary school that brings together young people from across Africa, providing them with a rigorous academic program that emphasizes leadership, entrepreneurship, and a commitment to ethical governance. The school's mission is to develop the next generation of African leaders who will take on the continent's most pressing challenges and drive transformation.

ALA's curriculum is uniquely African in focus, but it also incorporates global best practices in leadership education. By equipping students with practical skills in entrepreneurship and critical thinking, ALA aims to create a new class of young leaders who will have the confidence and expertise to lead Africa into a prosperous future. The success of ALA graduates, many of whom have gone on to launch social enterprises or take up leadership roles across Africa, speaks to the effectiveness of its model.

International Lessons: Finland and Singapore

While African countries are making strides in education, there are also valuable lessons to be drawn from international examples. Two of the world's most successful education systems—Finland and Singapore—offer key insights into how Africa can structure its reforms to meet the needs of a new era.

Chapter 3

1. Finland: A Focus on Equity and Teacher Empowerment

Finland consistently ranks near the top in global education rankings, thanks to its emphasis on educational equity and teacher quality. In Finland, teaching is a highly respected profession, and teachers are given significant autonomy to develop curricula that meet the needs of their students. The Finnish model prioritizes student well-being and holistic development over standardized testing, ensuring that students are prepared not only academically but also emotionally and socially.

One of the key takeaways from Finland's success is the importance of investing in teacher training and professional development. For

> …create teacher training programs that equip educators with both subject expertise and modern pedagogical techniques, ensuring that they can deliver high-quality education in both urban and rural contexts.

African nations, this could involve creating teacher training programs that equip educators with both subject expertise and modern pedagogical techniques, ensuring that they can deliver high-quality education in both urban and rural contexts. Africa's best can be found anywhere—rural or urban.

2. Singapore: A Model of Future-Ready Education

Singapore's educational system is widely regarded as one of the most innovative in the world. It has undergone continuous reform to ensure that students are prepared for the demands of a rapidly changing global economy. Singapore emphasizes STEM (science, technology, engineering, and mathematics) education, but it also recognizes the importance of critical thinking, creativity, and adaptability. The country has invested heavily in building a world-class educational infrastructure that includes cutting-edge technology and facilities.

For Africa, Singapore's approach underscores the need to develop future-ready educational systems that not only equip students with academic knowledge but also foster the skills needed for innovation and entrepreneurship. Africa's growing youth population can be an incredible asset if educational reforms focus on developing these future skills.

The Path Forward: A Vision for African Education

To build the leaders of tomorrow, African educational systems must be reimagined to address both current challenges and future needs. Several key elements will be essential to achieving this transformation:

1. Curriculum Reform

African countries must update their curricula to reflect the realities of the 21st century. This means incorporating critical thinking, problem-solving, and digital literacy into the core fundamentals. Curricula must also be contextualized to Africa's unique challenges, teaching students how to innovate and lead within their own communities.

2. Teacher Training and Empowerment

As demonstrated by Finland's success, investing in teachers is one of the most impactful ways to improve educational outcomes. African nations should prioritize teacher training and professional development, providing educators with the resources and support they need to thrive. Empowered teachers, in turn, will create more dynamic and engaging learning environments.

3. Investment in Technology

Technology is already transforming education across Africa, but there is potential for even greater impact. Governments and private sector stakeholders must work together to ensure that all students, regardless of location, have access to the digital tools that will prepare them for the future. Expanding internet access, building digital infrastructure, and promoting EdTech solutions will be critical to this effort.

4. Collaboration and Knowledge Sharing

African countries can accelerate their educational reforms by learning from one another and from successful models abroad. Collaboration across borders will allow for the exchange of best practices and the development of regionally tailored solutions that meet the diverse needs of Africa's students.

Conclusion

Africa's future depends on the education of its youth. By embracing innovative approaches to education—drawing inspiration from both African success stories and international models—the continent can grow a generation of leaders capable of driving sustainable development and prosperity.

Education for a new era must be forward-thinking, inclusive, and focused on preparing students not only for the challenges of today but for the opportunities of tomorrow. As this book continues, we will explore how governance and entrepreneurship can complement these educational reforms, creating an ecosystem in which Africa's youth can thrive and lead.

Chapter 4:
Governance and Accountability: Redefining Leadership in Africa

Introduction

Governance is the backbone of any nation's progress. For Africa, effective governance—paired with accountability—is essential to achieving sustainable development. Over the past few decades, many African nations have struggled with weak institutions, corruption, and a lack of transparency. These challenges have slowed economic growth, hindered social development, and eroded public trust in leadership. Yet today, Africa stands at a turning point. A generational shift in leadership—centered on integrity, transparency, and the rule of law—can redefine the continent's future.

This chapter explores how governance and accountability can be reimagined through

Chapter 4

> **Resource-rich African countries have often fallen victim to what has been called the "resource curse," a paradox whereby nations abundant in natural resources, including oil, diamonds, and minerals, experience stagnated or even declining economic growth.**

transformative leadership. Drawing on examples from Africa and around the world, it highlights how innovative models and principled leadership can foster development, restore public trust, and create more equitable societies.

Governance and Accountability in Africa: The Current Landscape

Africa's governance landscape is diverse. Some countries have made commendable strides in democratization, institutional reform, and transparency. Others continue to struggle with corruption, leadership crises, and fragile systems. The political environments in many African nations have been shaped by the legacies of colonialism, military rule, and authoritarian regimes—systems that often prioritized power consolidation over citizen service.

Resource-rich nations, in particular, face the paradox known as the resource curse—where abundance in natural wealth has fueled political instability, inequality, and economic stagnation. Rather than enabling development, revenues from oil, diamonds, and minerals have often enriched a narrow elite, while infrastructure, education, and healthcare remain underfunded. Over-reliance on resource extraction also makes these economies vulnerable to global price shocks, reinforcing cycles of instability.

In many cases, resource wealth becomes a source of power struggles, weakening governance and undermining democracy. Leaders may prioritize protecting control over natural resources instead of advancing long-term development or public accountability.

In Nigeria, oil wealth has fueled systemic corruption and mismanagement. The Niger Delta, rich in oil reserves, has experienced long-standing

Chapter 4

conflict involving local communities, militant groups, and government forces—all vying for control of revenues. While billions have been generated, much of the wealth has been siphoned by political elites, leaving many citizens in poverty. These dynamics have obstructed democratic progress and undermined public trust in leadership.

Angola offers another example. As one of Africa's largest oil producers, Angola has seen its resource wealth concentrated among the ruling elite. During and after the civil war (1975–2002), control of diamond mines became a tool of conflict and political survival. Even after peace was restored, oil revenues failed to translate into widespread development. The political class remained enriched, while much of the population continued to face poverty. This imbalance has weakened institutions and discouraged efforts toward accountable leadership.

Despite these challenges, several African nations have demonstrated that good governance and ethical leadership are not only possible—they are transformative. Countries like Botswana, Ghana, and Rwanda offer practical lessons in how leadership rooted in accountability can foster trust, drive economic development, and uplift citizens.

Botswana: Africa's Model of Democratic Stability

Botswana is often cited as one of Africa's most successful governance stories. Since gaining independence in 1966, the country has maintained a stable multiparty democracy, characterized by free elections, peaceful transitions of power, and institutional respect for the rule of law.

Central to Botswana's success is its responsible management of natural resources—particularly diamonds. Unlike many resource-rich nations, Botswana has used its diamond wealth to invest in national development. The government has prioritized healthcare, education, and infrastructure, ensuring that natural wealth benefits the broader population rather than a privileged few.

Chapter 4

Botswana's commitment to clean governance is supported by institutions like the Directorate on Corruption and Economic Crime (DCEC), which investigates and prosecutes corruption cases. These efforts have strengthened public trust and demonstrated how integrity in leadership can produce tangible improvements in people's lives. Today, Botswana enjoys a high Human Development Index (HDI) relative to other sub-Saharan African countries and is recognized as a model of principled leadership on the continent.

Rwanda: The Power of Leadership and Accountability

Rwanda's transformation over the past two decades provides a powerful example of how leadership can be redefined in the aftermath of conflict. Following the 1994 genocide, Rwanda was left economically and socially devastated. Under the leadership of President Paul Kagame, however, the country has experienced a remarkable recovery—prioritizing governance reform, national unity, and economic development.

Rwanda's governance model emphasizes accountability at every level. Institutions like the Rwanda Governance Board (RGB) monitor public sector performance to ensure effective service delivery. Additionally, the Imihigo performance contracts—signed between the president and local officials—set clear development targets, and leaders are held accountable for achieving them. This results-driven culture has led to visible improvements in infrastructure, healthcare, education, and security.

While Rwanda's model has been praised for its efficiency and low levels of corruption, it has also drawn criticism for its restrictions on political freedoms. Nevertheless, the country's success in reducing poverty, advancing gender equality, and fostering development underscores the impact of strong, accountable leadership.

Chapter 4

Ghana: Strengthening Democratic Institutions

Ghana is another African success story in democratic governance and institutional accountability. Since transitioning from military rule to democracy in 1992, Ghana has established one of the most vibrant democratic systems on the continent. Regular elections, peaceful transfers of power, and a strong civil society have earned Ghana its reputation as a beacon of democracy in West Africa.

Key to this success has been the creation of independent institutions such as the Commission on Human Rights and Administrative Justice (CHRAJ) and the Office of the Auditor-General, which play vital roles in combating corruption and holding public officials accountable. Ghana also boasts one of Africa's freest media landscapes, with journalists actively investigating and exposing misconduct.

Ghana's experience shows that strong institutions, paired with an active civil society, are essential to maintaining public trust and ensuring government accountability. Its commitment to free elections, political openness, and rule of law continues to serve as a model for other African nations.

Lessons from the Global Stage: Singapore and Estonia

In addition to African examples, there are important lessons from the global stage. Countries like Singapore and Estonia stand out for their innovative approaches to governance and rapid development, driven by effective leadership and a deep commitment to accountability.

Singapore: From Poverty to Prosperity through Governance

Singapore's transformation from a struggling post-colonial city-state into one of the world's most prosperous nations illustrates the power of visionary leadership. Under Prime Minister Lee Kuan Yew, Singapore prioritized clean governance, efficiency, and meritocracy. Institutions like the Public Service Commission

Chapter 4

and the Corrupt Practices Investigation Bureau (CPIB) played a central role in selecting competent civil servants and rooting out corruption.

Lee's leadership was grounded in the principle that governments must be accountable to their citizens and produce tangible results. His administration emphasized long-term planning, education reform, and infrastructure investment — laying the foundation for sustained economic growth.

Singapore's experience demonstrates how building strong, transparent institutions and prioritizing public service can transform a nation. For African countries, it offers a powerful blueprint for leadership grounded in integrity and performance.

Estonia: E-Governance and Accountability

Estonia, a small Baltic nation, has become a global leader in digital governance. After gaining independence from the Soviet Union in 1991, Estonia invested heavily in technology to rebuild its economy and public institutions. The result is a cutting-edge e-governance platform that has made government services more transparent, accessible, and efficient.

Through its e-Estonia initiative, citizens can vote, pay taxes, register businesses, and access services online. This digital transformation has dramatically reduced opportunities for corruption and increased public trust. It has also improved access to government services and created a more responsive and inclusive public sector.

For Africa, Estonia's model highlights the transformative potential of digital innovation in governance. By investing in digital infrastructure, African nations can enhance transparency, reduce bureaucracy, and foster citizen engagement.

The Path Forward: Redefining Leadership in Africa

Redefining leadership is one of the most urgent generational shifts Africa must undertake. This transformation requires a multifaceted approach that prioritizes good governance, institutional

Chapter 4

strength, and public accountability. Key strategies include:

1. Strengthening Democratic Institutions

African nations must invest in building independent institutions—such as electoral commissions, anti-corruption bodies, and judicial systems—that can hold public officials accountable and safeguard democratic processes.

2. Promoting Civic Engagement

Governments should create environments that encourage public participation. Civic engagement empowers citizens to act as watchdogs and contributes to a culture of accountability and transparency.

3. Leveraging Technology for Accountability

Digital infrastructure can dramatically improve service delivery and reduce corruption. E-governance platforms, modeled after Estonia's, can foster transparency and trust between governments and their citizens.

4. Developing Leadership Training Programs

Africa's next generation of leaders must be equipped with both the skills and ethical grounding to lead with integrity. Programs like the African Leadership Academy can help nurture principled, forward-thinking leaders across the continent.

Conclusion

Governance and accountability are cornerstones of Africa's long-term development. This chapter has highlighted successful leadership models from both African and global contexts, demonstrating that effective governance is not only possible—it is already happening.

By redefining leadership to emphasize service, integrity, and results, African nations can unlock their full potential and secure a prosperous, inclusive future for all. In the chapters ahead, we will explore how entrepreneurship and economic empowerment can work hand-in-hand with governance reforms to drive Africa's transformation.

Chapter 5:
Entrepreneurship and Economic Freedom: Creating a Path to Prosperity

Introduction

Entrepreneurship is a key driver of economic growth and job creation. For Africa, it holds the promise of unlocking unprecedented prosperity. With one of the youngest populations in the world and a rapidly growing digital landscape, the continent is primed for a surge in entrepreneurial activity—empowering individuals, generating employment, and building resilient local economies.

However, to fully harness the power of entrepreneurship, African nations must confront systemic barriers such as limited access to capital, inadequate infrastructure, and restrictive regulatory environments that hinder innovation and economic freedom.

This chapter explores how entrepreneurship—supported by economic freedom—can serve as a pathway to prosperity. Drawing on success stories from across Africa and beyond, we will examine how enabling environments and strategic investment in entrepreneurs can lead to lasting economic transformation and greater self-reliance for the continent.

The Role of Entrepreneurship in Africa's Economic Future

Africa's economic future lies not only in its natural resources, but in the creativity and resilience of its people. Entrepreneurship is already reshaping key sectors including agriculture, technology, manufacturing, and services. Small and medium-sized enterprises (SMEs) form the backbone of many African economies, accounting for approximately 80 percent of jobs across the continent.

Chapter 5

Despite this significance, many aspiring entrepreneurs face persistent obstacles: limited access to finance, weak infrastructure, and overly rigid regulatory systems.

To fully unleash Africa's entrepreneurial potential, there must be a shift away from overly centralized, government-led development models. Instead, nations should focus on empowering individuals and communities to take control of their economic futures. By fostering environments where businesses can thrive, governments can support a new generation of entrepreneurs—driving innovation, job creation, and economic resilience.

Success Stories in African Entrepreneurship

Across the continent, several countries are embracing entrepreneurship as a cornerstone of economic growth. By leveraging innovation, digital tools, and human capital, a wave of African entrepreneurs is rising to meet both local needs and global opportunities.

1. Kenya: The Silicon Savannah

Kenya has earned the nickname "Silicon Savannah" due to its booming tech sector. The country is home to M-Pesa, one of the world's most successful mobile money platforms, which has transformed financial inclusion by providing millions with access to financial services via mobile phones. M-Pesa's success has catalyzed a wave of digital innovation, positioning Nairobi as a startup hub for fintech, agritech, and e-commerce.

Kenya's government has played a key role in enabling this ecosystem—investing in ICT infrastructure and offering tax incentives to tech startups. Supported by accelerators, venture capital, and public-private initiatives, Kenya's entrepreneurial landscape demonstrates how technology and policy alignment can fuel economic growth and improve quality of life.

Chapter 5

2. Nigeria: A Hub for Creative Industries and Technology

Nigeria's entrepreneurial energy shines through its dynamic creative sector and growing tech ecosystem. Nollywood, the country's film industry, is the second-largest in the world by production volume and generates substantial local and international revenue.

Meanwhile, Nigeria's fintech scene is thriving, with companies like Flutterwave and Paystack revolutionizing online payments, facilitating cross-border commerce, and attracting major venture capital investment.

Nigeria's entrepreneurial momentum is driven by a large domestic market, access to capital, and global collaboration. However, challenges such as poor infrastructure and regulatory complexity remain. Addressing these barriers will be essential to fully realizing the country's entrepreneurial potential.

3. Liberia: J-Palm Liberia's Leading Example of Social Enterprise in Africa

J-Palm Liberia is a compelling example of how social enterprises in Africa can tackle pressing social and environmental challenges while driving economic growth. Founded in 2013 by Mahmud Johnson, J-Palm has transformed Liberia's palm oil sector by offering innovative solutions to long-standing issues in agriculture, rural poverty, and sustainability. The company demonstrates how a mission-driven business model can empower communities and improve livelihoods—while remaining commercially viable.

At the core of J-Palm's model is the value-added use of palm kernel oil, a byproduct often discarded in traditional production. By creating products under the *Kernel Fresh* line—natural beauty and skincare items made from palm kernel oil—J-Palm has tapped into a previously overlooked resource, enhancing sustainability and efficiency in the supply chain.

The enterprise works closely with smallholder farmers, many of whom depend on

Chapter 5

traditional palm oil production for their livelihoods. J-Palm supplies simple, effective tools like portable processing machines, which boost oil extraction efficiency and reduce waste. This partnership increases farmers' incomes and minimizes environmental impact by discouraging deforestation and overexploitation of land.

To ensure market access and promote local job creation, J-Palm has built a direct-to-consumer sales network using grassroots sales representatives. This approach makes Kernel Fresh products widely available while creating income-generating opportunities—especially for youth and women.

Since its founding, J-Palm Liberia has made a substantial impact, increasing smallholder farmer incomes by up to 80 percent through improved production and direct-purchase agreements. The company has turned traditional farming into a more profitable and sustainable venture, helping rural communities break cycles of poverty and achieve economic empowerment.

On the consumer side, Kernel Fresh products are now widely popular in Liberia, valued for their quality and affordability. J-Palm has also expanded into neighboring markets, positioning itself as a regional leader in natural skincare. Its commitment to community impact and environmental sustainability has earned it recognition from international organizations such as the United Nations Development Programme (UNDP) and other innovation platforms across Africa.

Founder Mahmud Johnson has become a respected voice in African entrepreneurship. His vision and leadership have inspired a new generation of business leaders to explore how enterprise can serve as a tool for social change. J-Palm Liberia exemplifies what's possible when African entrepreneurs build businesses that are profitable, sustainable, and purpose-driven.

Conclusion

J-Palm Liberia demonstrates the transformative power of social enterprise in Africa. By tackling

Chapter 5

inefficiency, environmental degradation, and rural poverty, the company has shown that business can be a tool for both development and empowerment. Its model—grounded in sustainability, social impact, and profitability—offers a blueprint for other entrepreneurs across the continent.

As Africa continues to explore new pathways for growth, enterprises like J-Palm are lighting the way forward. Their success shows that when local resources are leveraged, communities are empowered, and innovation is prioritized, lasting change is not only possible—it's already happening.

Removing Barriers: The Importance of Economic Freedom

While Africa's entrepreneurial landscape shows great promise, significant barriers to economic freedom still limit its full potential. Economic freedom refers to the ability of individuals to control their labor and property. For entrepreneurs, this means the freedom to start and grow businesses without excessive government interference.

According to GlobalEconomy.com and various economic freedom indexes, many African countries continue to rank low due to factors such as overregulation, corruption, and weak rule of law. However, there are exceptions. Countries like Mauritius, Botswana, Seychelles, and Rwanda are leading the continent with higher rankings, driven by reforms that promote freer markets and more transparent governance.

For entrepreneurship to truly thrive, African governments must pursue economic reforms that reduce bureaucratic red tape, simplify business registration, ensure property rights, and improve transparency. Equally important is access to affordable financing. Many entrepreneurs struggle to obtain loans or attract investment due to underdeveloped financial sectors and lack of credit support.

Countries that have made progress in improving economic freedom have also experienced noticeable entrepreneurial growth.

Chapter 5

Mauritius, for instance, is consistently ranked among the top African nations for economic freedom. Through reforms aimed at improving the ease of doing business, reducing corruption, and fostering a competitive tax environment, Mauritius has become a magnet for investment and entrepreneurship—especially in finance and tourism.

Lessons from Outside Africa: The Power of Economic Freedom in Driving Entrepreneurship

While Africa's progress is promising, valuable lessons can also be drawn from other parts of the world where economic freedom has played a key role in national development.

1. South Korea: From Post-War Poverty to Economic Miracle

South Korea's rise from post-war poverty in the 1950s to becoming one of the world's leading economies is often cited as a model of entrepreneurial success. Critical to its transformation was the government's investment in education, infrastructure, and policies that supported small and medium-sized enterprises (SMEs).

By promoting innovation and maintaining a business-friendly regulatory environment, South Korea enabled the growth of global giants like Samsung, Hyundai, and LG—companies that all began as small entrepreneurial ventures. The country's emphasis on education, R&D, and intellectual property rights helped position its entrepreneurs for global competitiveness—a path that African nations can study and adapt.

2. Chile: Creating an Entrepreneurial Hub in Latin America

Chile has developed one of Latin America's most dynamic entrepreneurial ecosystems. This progress was fueled by economic reforms focused on liberalizing markets, reducing government interference, and encouraging foreign investment.

The Start-Up Chile program, launched in 2010, offers equity-free grants to entrepreneurs worldwide, inviting them to build their businesses

Chapter 5

in Chile. This initiative has helped position Chile as a regional hub for innovation and technology startups.

Chile's experience illustrates how supportive government-led programs—combined with economic freedom—can empower entrepreneurs and drive growth in key sectors such as technology, agriculture, and renewable energy.

Empowering African Entrepreneurs Through Education and Skills Development

While economic freedom and policy reform are essential, education and skills development are equally important for nurturing Africa's next generation of entrepreneurs. Many young Africans still lack access to quality education, vocational training, and entrepreneurial know-how.

Governments, the private sector, and academic institutions must collaborate to close this gap. Programs focusing on financial literacy, business management, and technical skills can help build the foundation for a thriving entrepreneurial culture.

Rwanda has already taken steps in this direction. Its YouthConnekt program provides young people with entrepreneurship training and mentorship—equipping them to build viable businesses and contribute to national development. Similar efforts across the continent could help unlock the full potential of Africa's youth and fuel inclusive economic growth.

Conclusion

Entrepreneurship and economic freedom are the twin engines of Africa's future prosperity. As this chapter has shown, nurturing a culture of entrepreneurship—supported by reforms that promote market freedom and innovation—can drive transformative change across the continent.

By removing barriers to economic freedom, expanding access to capital, and investing in education and skills development, African nations can create environments where entrepreneurs

Chapter 5

thrive, new industries emerge, and long-term growth takes root.

As we move forward, the next chapter will explore the social and environmental dimensions of Africa's development—with a focus on how innovation and entrepreneurship can advance sustainability for both people and the planet. In this era of generational shift, Africa's entrepreneurs hold the key to unlocking economic freedom and prosperity for generations to come.

Chapter 6:
Righteousness and Justice: The Call for Moral and Just Leadership

Introduction

Central to the teachings of the Bible are the principles of righteousness and justice, which form the foundation of moral leadership and societal harmony. *Psalm 89:14* declares, "Righteousness and justice are the foundation of your throne; steadfast love and faithfulness go before you." This verse reveals the divine blueprint for leadership—one built on the pillars of righteousness (right living and moral integrity) and justice (fairness and equity). These values are essential not only to personal conduct but to the structures that shape entire nations.

For Africa to break the cycles of corruption, inequality, and oppression, these biblical principles must be woven into the moral fabric of its leadership and governance.

Chapter 6

This chapter explores the biblical foundation of righteousness and justice, drawing on scripture to demonstrate their importance in promoting authentic leadership, societal equality, and national flourishing. It also reflects on how these principles can guide African nations toward moral renewal, sustainable development, and peace.

The Biblical Foundation of Righteousness and Justice

Psalm 89:14 presents righteousness and justice as the very foundation of God's rule—implying that without these pillars, leadership cannot truly stand. Righteousness, in biblical terms, means living in alignment with God's will—doing what is right, just, and pure. Justice refers to fairness and equity, ensuring that all individuals, regardless of status, are treated fairly and that wrongs are corrected.

Proverbs 21:3 says, "To do righteousness and justice is more acceptable to the Lord than sacrifice." This verse emphasizes that God values ethical conduct and fairness over religious ritual. Leaders and citizens alike are called to live by these principles in both public and private life. This teaching has deep relevance in African contexts where corruption, inequality, and injustice have hindered growth and social cohesion. Leaders who embody righteousness and justice cultivate trust, integrity, and fairness—conditions essential for lasting development.

The prophet Amos delivers a powerful vision for justice in *Amos 5:24*: "But let justice roll down like waters, and righteousness like an ever-flowing stream." This is not a call for temporary reforms, but for a continuous outpouring of justice that permeates every corner of society. In African nations struggling with systemic injustice, Amos' words challenge the status quo and call for a moral revolution—a generational shift rooted in fairness and integrity.

Justice as the Heart of Good Governance

The Bible consistently links justice with peace and national stability. Leaders are expected to uphold

Chapter 6

justice as a reflection of God's character. *Proverbs 29:4* affirms this: "By justice a king gives a country stability, but those who are greedy for bribes tear it down." Justice, then, is not merely an abstract principle—it is a stabilizing force for nations. Corruption, bribery, and self-interest, on the other hand, destroy institutions from within.

In many African nations, the erosion of public trust due to corruption has undermined institutions and stalled development. Biblical justice, however, is not only about punishing wrongdoing—it involves creating systems and conditions in which all people can thrive. *Isaiah 1:17* urges: "Learn to do right; seek justice. Defend the oppressed. Take up the cause of the fatherless; plead the case of the widow." Justice, in this sense, is proactive and protective, especially for the vulnerable.

This broader view of justice encompasses economic, social, and political dimensions—ensuring fairness in education, healthcare, economic opportunity, and access to resources. Leaders committed to biblical justice will work to build inclusive systems that reject favoritism, nepotism, and inequality. Countries that pursue this form of justice tend to experience more sustainable and inclusive development, as the benefits of growth are distributed equitably.

Righteousness as the Moral Compass for Leadership

Righteousness in leadership is about moral integrity—leading with honesty, accountability, humility, and respect for others. In Africa, as elsewhere, leadership often falters when integrity is compromised through greed, abuse of power, or ethical negligence.

Proverbs 16:12 says, "It is an abomination for kings to commit wickedness, for a throne is established by righteousness." Leadership built on wrongdoing is unstable and unsustainable. But leadership grounded in righteousness fosters trust, builds stable societies, and creates environments where individuals can pursue their potential with dignity and purpose.

Chapter 6

Righteousness also guides how leaders treat others—in governance, business, and everyday life. *Micah 6:8* captures the essence of righteous leadership: "He has shown you, O mortal, what is good. And what does the Lord require of you? To act justly and to love mercy and to walk humbly with your God." Leaders who embody these values cultivate a culture of fairness, compassion, and mutual respect.

In a continent seeking transformation, righteous and just leadership is not just a moral ideal—it is a practical necessity. Leaders who commit to these values lay the foundation for peace, progress, and prosperity that reaches across generations.

Chapter 7:
Social Justice and Inclusion: Bridging the Gaps

Introduction

Africa's potential for growth and prosperity cannot be fully realized without addressing the deep-rooted inequalities and systemic exclusion that have characterized many of its societies. Social justice and inclusion are essential components of sustainable development, ensuring that all individuals—regardless of gender, ethnicity, disability, or economic status—have equal opportunities to participate in and benefit from progress.

For Africa to thrive in this new era, there must be a collective commitment to bridging the gaps that have long marginalized certain groups and to creating a more just, equitable, and inclusive society.

Chapter 7

This chapter explores the importance of social justice and inclusion in Africa's generational shift and how these principles can be integrated into political, economic, and social systems to build a fairer future. Drawing on examples from both within Africa and globally, we'll examine how inclusive policies and social movements can drive change, foster unity, and bridge the divides that hold nations back.

The Effects of Tribalism in African Societies

Tribalism, while rooted in Africa's cultural and historical identity, has often served as a source of division in modern African nations. During colonial rule, European powers deliberately exploited ethnic differences, using a "divide and rule" strategy that entrenched tribal rivalries. After independence, many nations struggled to forge a unified identity, with tribal affiliations continuing to influence political loyalties and access to public resources.

Generational Shift

In some cases, this has led to political instability, as leaders have used ethnic loyalty to maintain power, resulting in marginalization, social tension, and a lack of national cohesion. In extreme cases, tribalism has fueled violence—as seen in the 1994 Rwandan genocide, where long-standing divisions between Hutus and Tutsis led to catastrophic loss of life.

Beyond violent conflict, tribalism undermines development by creating systems where nepotism, favoritism, and exclusion thrive. In many countries, access to jobs, education, and government positions is determined more by tribal affiliation than by merit. This not only alienates minority groups but also erodes institutional trust and limits national unity. Economic progress is hindered when division restricts equitable access to opportunities and prevents the formation of a shared national vision.

Addressing tribalism requires a multifaceted approach that promotes inclusivity, justice, and a commitment to the collective good over narrow ethnic interests. One important

Chapter 7

strategy is fostering national unity through education and media—promoting shared values, national narratives, and civic identity while honoring cultural diversity.

Institutional reforms are also vital. These include ensuring fair political representation, equitable distribution of resources, and policies that protect the rights of minority and marginalized communities. Systems like proportional representation in governance can help avoid the concentration of power within a single group.

Several African nations have taken steps to address tribal divisions and promote inclusion:

- **Rwanda**, post-genocide, banned public identification by ethnicity and promoted a unified national identity.

- **Ghana** has worked to ensure ethnic balance in government representation, supported by its multiparty democratic system.

- **South Africa's** Truth and Reconciliation Commission helped the nation confront racial and ethnic divisions, laying a foundation for healing and dialogue.

These examples demonstrate that with intentional policies and courageous leadership, African countries can overcome the divisive effects of tribalism and move toward cohesive, inclusive societies.

Understanding Social Justice and Inclusion in Africa

Social justice in Africa is not a new concept, but it has often been overshadowed by more immediate economic and political concerns. Colonialism and post-independence turmoil left behind systems marked by inequality, ethnic stratification, and gender imbalance. In many cases, these systemic issues remain unaddressed, keeping large portions of the population marginalized and excluded from development.

Social justice focuses on correcting these structural imbalances—ensuring that all people are treated fairly, protected under the law, and

Chapter 7

have access to the resources and rights needed to thrive.

Inclusion, however, takes this further. It emphasizes *active participation*—making sure that all individuals, particularly the most vulnerable, are not just protected but are fully engaged in the life of society. True inclusion breaks down the barriers that prevent people from accessing education, healthcare, economic opportunities, political representation, and civic engagement.

Barriers to inclusion often stem from poverty, discrimination, disability, gender bias, and lack of access to essential services. These must be addressed at every level—through policies that intentionally empower marginalized groups and through cultural shifts that challenge exclusionary mindsets.

For Africa to fully realize its generational shift, these issues must be addressed head-on. This means:

- Confronting historical injustices and healing past grievances

- Reforming institutions to be more accessible, accountable, and equitable
- Empowering communities through education, grassroots development, and representation
- Designing systems that allow all citizens—regardless of background—to participate in and benefit from national growth

Inclusive societies are stronger, more stable, and more innovative. By making justice and inclusion core priorities, African nations can unlock the full potential of their people and chart a new path toward unity and shared prosperity.

The Importance of Gender Equality in Social Justice

One of the most urgent issues in Africa's pursuit of social justice is gender inequality. While notable progress has been made in recent years, women in many parts of the continent still face significant barriers to education, healthcare, political participation, and economic opportunity. In some regions, outdated cultural practices and restrictive

Chapter 7

legal frameworks continue to marginalize women, denying them fundamental rights and freedoms.

Rwanda stands out as a global leader in gender equality. In the aftermath of the 1994 genocide, Rwanda's leadership recognized the critical role women would play in rebuilding the nation. Today, women hold more than 60 percent of seats in the country's parliament—among the highest rates of female representation in the world. Rwanda has also implemented gender-responsive policies that promote women's access to education, healthcare, and economic empowerment.

The success of Rwanda's gender equality movement illustrates that when women are fully included in society, the entire nation benefits. By addressing the systemic exclusion of women, Rwanda has not only closed social gaps but has also created a more inclusive and equitable society—one that can serve as a model for the rest of the continent.

Inclusion of Marginalized Ethnic Groups

Ethnic diversity is one of Africa's greatest assets, but when not managed carefully, it can also become a source of conflict. From the Rwandan genocide to ongoing tensions in South Sudan, the failure to build inclusive societies has often led to devastating consequences. Bridging ethnic divides is essential to fostering peace, promoting stability, and creating an environment in which all individuals can thrive.

Ethiopia's federal system, based on ethnic representation, offers a unique example. Its constitution acknowledges the right of ethnic groups to self-governance and cultural preservation, allowing a degree of autonomy that has helped manage diversity. Although Ethiopia has recently faced ethnic-related conflicts, its approach highlights the importance of institutional inclusion in addressing long-standing divisions.

Still, inclusion must extend beyond politics. True social justice requires that marginalized

Chapter 7

ethnic groups have equal access to education, healthcare, and economic opportunity. Whether rooted in language, geography, or culture, the causes of exclusion must be identified and addressed. Building inclusive societies demands structural reforms that empower every citizen, regardless of their ethnic background.

Economic Inclusion: Tackling Poverty and Inequality

Economic exclusion remains one of the most pressing challenges to social justice in Africa. In many rural and underserved communities, people are trapped in cycles of poverty with limited access to essential services such as clean water, healthcare, and quality education. This not only hampers personal progress—it undermines national development.

Inclusive economic policies focused on poverty reduction and wealth redistribution are essential. Botswana provides a positive example. Through responsible management of its diamond resources, Botswana has invested heavily in public goods like education, healthcare, and infrastructure. Programs such as free primary education and universal healthcare have helped reduce poverty and promote shared growth.

In Ghana, the government's Livelihood Empowerment Against Poverty (LEAP) program has targeted the most vulnerable populations. By providing cash transfers to poor households, the program improves access to basic services and helps reduce intergenerational poverty. These kinds of targeted efforts are vital in ensuring that economic growth results in broad-based benefits— not just gains for the wealthy or politically connected.

Inclusion of Persons with Disabilities

Another key area of social exclusion in Africa is the marginalization of persons with disabilities (PWDs). Across the continent, people with disabilities often face barriers to education, employment, healthcare, and public services. Discriminatory attitudes and inaccessible environments frequently leave them on the

Chapter 7

margins of society—underrepresented, unheard, and underserved.

South Africa has taken steps to address this gap through comprehensive legal and policy frameworks. Its Promotion of Equality and Prevention of Unfair Discrimination Act prohibits discrimination based on disability. The government has made progress in improving accessibility in public buildings, education, and transportation.

In addition, organizations like Sightsavers and the Africa Disability Alliance are leading advocacy efforts to ensure that PWDs are included in decision-making processes and protected under the law.

Ensuring justice for persons with disabilities means building inclusive environments where everyone—regardless of ability—has equal access to opportunity. This involves investing in accessible infrastructure, advancing inclusive education, and changing public attitudes through awareness and education. Inclusion is not only a matter of rights—it's essential for building compassionate, cohesive, and forward-looking societies.

Lessons from Global Examples of Social Justice and Inclusion

While Africa is making significant strides in advancing social justice and inclusion, valuable lessons can be drawn from countries around the world that have implemented effective and innovative strategies to address inequality and promote social cohesion.

> ...empower marginalized communities, reduce inequality, and promote social justice.

1. **Brazil: Conditional Cash Transfers and Poverty Reduction**

Brazil's *Bolsa Família* program is one of the most successful examples of a conditional cash transfer initiative aimed at reducing poverty and promoting social inclusion. The program provides financial assistance to low-income families on the condition that they send their children to school and ensure they receive regular health checkups.

Chapter 7

Since its inception, *Bolsa Família* has lifted millions out of poverty and significantly improved education and health outcomes among Brazil's most vulnerable populations.

This model demonstrates how targeted social programs can empower marginalized communities, reduce inequality, and advance social justice. African nations can adapt similar approaches to combat extreme poverty and ensure that disadvantaged groups have access to essential services.

2. Norway: Gender Equality and Social Welfare

Norway consistently ranks among the most gender-equal countries in the world, largely due to its comprehensive social welfare system and commitment to gender equity. Policies on parental leave, affordable childcare, and equal pay have enabled both men and women to participate fully in the workforce and family life.

Norway's legal frameworks ensure that women's rights are protected and enforced, contributing to a culture of fairness and opportunity.

Its approach highlights the importance of comprehensive, rights-based social policies that support families, promote work-life balance, and address systemic gender inequalities. This offers an inspiring model for how legal protections and social investment can create inclusive, just societies.

The Path Forward: Bridging the Gaps in Africa

For Africa to achieve a generational shift, it must place social justice and inclusion at the heart of its development agenda. This means designing systems and policies that address historic inequalities and ensure all citizens are empowered to participate in the continent's progress.

Key areas of focus include:

1. Inclusive Governance and Representation

Governments must ensure that all citizens—regardless of ethnicity, gender, disability, or

Chapter 7

background—have a voice in decision-making. This requires building governance structures that reflect the diversity of African societies and intentionally addressing the historic marginalization of certain groups.

2. Economic Policies That Prioritize Inclusion

Inclusive economic growth must go beyond GDP figures. Policies should be crafted to reduce inequality, invest in vulnerable populations, and create opportunities for education, employment, and entrepreneurship. Social programs targeting the underserved can help close the wealth gap and build more resilient economies.

3. Legislation and Rights Protection

Strong legal frameworks are essential to protect the rights of women, ethnic minorities, persons with disabilities, and other marginalized groups. These laws must not only exist—they must be implemented and enforced, with clear accountability for discriminatory practices and systemic exclusion.

Conclusion

Social justice and inclusion are not just moral ideals—they are essential for Africa's sustainable development. By addressing inequality, bridging social divides, and fostering inclusive participation, African nations can build more just, unified, and prosperous societies.

The examples from both within Africa and abroad show that with political will, thoughtful policy, and community engagement, lasting change is possible. A generation rooted in justice and equity can unlock a future defined by shared prosperity and collective progress.

As this book continues, we will explore how innovation, youth engagement, and transformative leadership can accelerate this generational shift—ensuring Africa's future is one of unity, empowerment, and bold advancement for all.

Chapter 8:
African Youth as Catalysts – Empowering the Next Generation for Change

Introduction

In the quest for generational shift, no group is more significant, dynamic, or promising than Africa's youth. Young Africans make up the largest demographic on the continent and possess unprecedented potential to drive transformation. But for this potential to become lasting change, there must be a strategic commitment to empowering, educating, and equipping them to serve as catalysts for progress.

This chapter explores how youth empowerment can break entrenched cycles, usher in new ideas and solutions, and shift the mindsets needed to build Africa's future.

> "...young Africans represent the largest population demographic on the continent, wielding unprecedented potential to drive transformation and shape the continent's future."

Understanding the Youth Advantage

Africa's youth hold a unique advantage: they are less bound by the outdated mindsets and structural norms that have limited past generations. Their openness to new ideas, adaptability, and desire for progress make them ideal agents of change.

This generation is also the most digitally connected in history. Access to global information, networks, and success stories has expanded their worldview and inspired many to reimagine what is possible for Africa.

The "youth advantage" lies in their energy, fresh perspectives, and capacity for innovation.

Chapter 8

But for this advantage to be realized, societies must nurture their potential rather than suppress it.

Breaking the Cycle: Why Youth Empowerment Is Key

In many African societies, traditional hierarchies and systemic limitations sideline young people—limiting their roles in education, employment, and governance. This exclusion wastes valuable talent and reinforces stagnation.

Empowering youth challenges these systems. It transforms young people from passive recipients into active contributors—innovating, leading, and building solutions. Youth empowerment includes four key pillars: quality education, economic opportunity, inclusive governance, and mentorship.

1. Quality Education and Skills Development

Education is the foundation of empowerment, but many African systems still emphasize rote learning over critical thinking, creativity, and innovation. Reforming education to cultivate these skills is essential to producing the thinkers and problem-solvers Africa needs.

Example: In Kenya, *AkiraChix* trains young women in coding, entrepreneurship, and technology. Their model builds not only individual skills but a tech-savvy workforce capable of driving innovation.

2. Economic Empowerment and Job Creation

With high youth unemployment across the continent, economic inclusion is crucial. Governments and the private sector must collaborate to support youth entrepreneurship, small business development, and job creation through funding, mentorship, and training.

Example: The *Tony Elumelu Foundation* provides funding, mentorship, and training to thousands of young entrepreneurs across Africa — cultivating a generation of self-reliant innovators and job creators.

3. Youth Representation in Governance

Policies that ignore youth concerns are often outdated or ineffective. Including young voices in political processes ensures that leadership reflects the needs of the majority demographic.

Example: *Rwanda* has made notable strides in youth representation, integrating young leaders into policy-making and strengthening responsiveness to youth concerns.

4. Mentorship and Role Models

Access to mentors is vital for personal and professional growth. Mentors help youth navigate challenges, offer practical advice, and provide encouragement that sustains momentum for change.

The Role of Technology in Youth Empowerment

Technology has become a powerful equalizer—giving young Africans tools to access knowledge, build networks, and launch change initiatives. From activism to entrepreneurship, the digital landscape is expanding what is possible.

Generational Shift

1. Social Media as a Tool for Activism

Social media empowers youth to bypass traditional media gatekeepers and speak directly to national and global audiences. Platforms like X, Instagram, and Facebook have amplified youth voices and allowed for rapid mobilization.

Example: The *#EndSARS* movement in Nigeria was a youth-led campaign against police brutality that gained momentum through social media. It galvanized national protests, sparked international solidarity, and showcased the power of digital organizing.

2. Tech Innovation and Entrepreneurship

Young Africans are also leveraging technology to build solutions for local problems—creating startups in fintech, edtech, health, and commerce. These ventures boost economies and demonstrate African ingenuity on the world stage.

Example: *Flutterwave,* co-founded by Nigerian entrepreneur Iyinoluwa Aboyeji, revolutionized digital payments across Africa. It not only simplified transactions but also

Chapter 8

empowered African businesses to engage in global commerce.

Cultivating a Culture of Youth-led Change

Empowering Africa's youth goes beyond policy reform and economic opportunity. It also requires a fundamental shift in how societies perceive youth leadership and innovation. Creating a culture that encourages risk-taking, values young voices, and celebrates local success stories can inspire future generations to lead with confidence and creativity.

Building a Culture of Inclusivity

True inclusivity means more than just symbolic representation. It involves embedding youth perspectives at the heart of policymaking and encouraging them to challenge outdated norms. When young people are included in national dialogues—on the economy, healthcare, governance, and the environment—they feel seen, heard, and valued.

Programs that integrate youth into policy discussions send a clear message: their contributions matter.

Recognizing and Celebrating Young Role Models

African cultures have traditionally revered elders as symbols of wisdom—a value that remains important. However, in today's rapidly evolving world, it's equally vital to celebrate young achievers who are breaking boundaries across fields—from science and entrepreneurship to activism and the arts.

Highlighting their stories signals to other young people that success, innovation, and leadership are not bound by age.

Conclusion: A Future Built by Youth

Africa's generational transformation depends on its youth—the most dynamic, connected, and visionary generation the continent has ever known. They hold the power not just to imagine a better future, but to build it.

Chapter 8

By breaking down structural barriers, fostering inclusive leadership, and nurturing innovation, we prepare a generation that will not only participate in their societies—but lead them.

To truly transform Africa, we must shift how we see the youth: not simply as the leaders of tomorrow, but as the change-makers of today. Their energy, passion, and resilience can redefine Africa's present and chart a bold course for its future.

The time is now to empower this generation—to give them the tools, trust, and space to create a continent that is resilient, inclusive, and future-ready. A continent whose brightest days lie ahead because it was shaped by its youth.

Chapter 9:
Capital Escape – Curbing Financial Flight from African Economies

Introduction

Capital flight—the large-scale exodus of financial resources from African nations—remains one of the continent's most pressing economic challenges. Every year, billions of dollars are siphoned out through both illicit means and legal but strategically disadvantageous investments abroad.

This chapter examines the underlying drivers of capital escape, the long-term consequences for African development, and the reforms necessary to retain financial resources and promote sustainable growth.

Understanding Capital Escape in Africa

Capital escape occurs when wealth generated within African economies flows outward—often into offshore accounts, foreign investments, or

Chapter 9

overseas properties. While some capital movement is a natural part of global economic activity, the **scale and structure** of Africa's capital flight are excessive and economically harmful.

This outflow deprives local economies of essential resources—funds that could be invested in infrastructure, healthcare, education, innovation, and job creation.

Key Drivers of Capital Escape in Africa

1. Weak Financial Institutions

A lack of transparency, poor oversight, and weak regulatory frameworks enable capital flight. In environments where institutions lack accountability, individuals and corporations can more easily exploit loopholes or move money illicitly without detection or consequence.

2. Corruption and Illicit Financial Flows

Corruption—both in public offices and the private sector—fuels capital flight. Bribery, embezzlement, and money laundering allow wealth to be extracted from national economies with impunity.

3. Tax Evasion and Avoidance by Multinational Corporations

Many multinational corporations operating in Africa use aggressive tax avoidance strategies such as transfer pricing—artificially shifting profits to low-tax jurisdictions. These practices deprive African governments of critical revenue that could otherwise be used for public development.

Compounding this issue is corruption among negotiators and regulators. Over the years, numerous deals involving natural resources, infrastructure, and trade have been shaped by personal interests and bribes. Multinational firms often offer "sweetheart deals" to gain favorable terms, while local officials prioritize personal gain over national benefit.

This has led to the extraction of Africa's most valuable assets—minerals, oil, timber—with minimal return for the local population. The consequences have compounded over time,

Chapter 9

exacerbating poverty instead of enabling prosperity.

Beyond financial loss, these compromised agreements damage public trust and erode the credibility of African institutions. When environmental, safety, and labor regulations are ignored in exchange for bribes, citizens suffer—not only through poor services and environmental harm, but through disillusionment with their governments.

Even worse, these deals entrench Africa's dependence on external powers. Instead of using their resources to build self-sustaining economies, many African nations remain stuck in cycles of exporting raw materials cheaply and importing finished goods at high prices—deepening trade deficits.

Breaking this cycle requires:

- Strengthening systems of accountability
- Promoting ethical leadership

- Ensuring that Africa's negotiators act in the public interest, not personal enrichment

4. Political Instability and Economic Insecurity

When businesses and individuals perceive political or economic instability, they seek to protect their wealth in more secure environments abroad. This triggers a self-reinforcing cycle: the flight of capital weakens local economies, which in turn deepens instability and discourages reinvestment.

5. Inadequate Domestic Investment Opportunities

A lack of viable investment opportunities at home also drives capital flight. When local markets are underdeveloped, inefficient, or perceived as risky, investors look elsewhere—robbing the continent of capital that could otherwise spur economic innovation, infrastructure growth, and entrepreneurship.

Chapter 9

Local Innovations and Social Enterprises as Catalysts for Investment

Local innovation, entrepreneurship, and social enterprises present powerful tools to counter capital flight and promote homegrown development. By leveraging indigenous knowledge and resources, Africans can create tailored solutions that address local challenges while building sustainable, scalable systems.

Social enterprises offer dual value: they generate profit and address urgent social needs — whether access to clean water, education, or affordable healthcare. Supporting such ventures through targeted policies, tax incentives, and access to capital empowers communities to invest in their own development.

This approach reduces reliance on foreign aid, fosters economic resilience, and nurtures a sense of ownership and accountability — key elements for long-term progress.

The Impact of Capital Escape on African Economies

The consequences of capital flight are wide-reaching and deeply damaging. Its effects can be seen across critical areas of economic development:

1. Loss of Public Revenue and Increased Debt

Capital flight erodes the tax base, as profits are hidden or relocated abroad to avoid taxation. This loss of revenue forces many African nations to rely on foreign aid or loans, resulting in ballooning debt and ongoing financial dependency.

2. Undermined Investment in Public Services

Funds that could support healthcare, education, and infrastructure are lost through capital escape. With fewer resources, governments struggle to deliver essential services—leaving communities vulnerable and underdeveloped.

3. Inhibited Private Sector Growth

The outflow of capital reduces available funds for local businesses and entrepreneurs. This weakens the private sector, stifles innovation, and limits job creation—slowing the emergence of strong, competitive African enterprises.

4. Erosion of Trust in African Financial Institutions

Persistent capital flight damages public confidence in local financial systems and government institutions. This erosion of trust makes it harder to attract investment, both locally and globally, as perceptions of instability and risk grow.

Strategies to Curb Capital Escape

Addressing capital flight requires a comprehensive, multi-layered strategy targeting its root causes while cultivating systems that promote accountability, investment, and transparency.

1. Strengthening Financial Institutions and Regulatory Frameworks

Transparent and accountable financial systems are essential to stopping capital flight. Governments must invest in regulatory oversight, enforce anti-money laundering laws, and eliminate opportunities for illicit financial flows.

Example: *South Africa* has strengthened its regulatory frameworks, introducing harsher penalties for companies involved in illicit flows. These measures have improved investor confidence and reduced outflows.

2. Promoting Tax Transparency and Reform

African countries should adopt international tax transparency standards and close loopholes that allow profit shifting. Participation in initiatives like the *OECD's Base Erosion and Profit Shifting (BEPS)* project can help stem tax avoidance by multinational corporations.

3. Leveraging Technology for Financial Surveillance

Advanced digital tools such as blockchain, AI, and data analytics can improve the monitoring of financial transactions. These technologies help identify suspicious patterns and prevent illicit outflows.

Chapter 9

Example: *Rwanda's digital taxation system* tracks transactions in real time, reducing tax evasion and increasing transparency in domestic financial activity.

4. Strengthening Local Investment Opportunities

Creating an attractive local investment climate is essential. This includes improving infrastructure, supporting sectors like agriculture and manufacturing, and offering incentives for local entrepreneurship. A vibrant domestic economy can retain capital and stimulate reinvestment.

5. Encouraging Diaspora Investment

Africans in the diaspora represent a valuable source of capital and expertise. Governments can tap into this potential through targeted policies and investment vehicles.

Example: *Ethiopia's Diaspora Bond* enables expatriates to invest in national infrastructure, channeling capital back into productive domestic projects.

Fostering a Culture of Accountability and Good Governance

Beyond technical solutions, addressing capital escape requires a cultural and ethical shift—one that embeds accountability and transparency into every level of leadership and business.

1. Anti-Corruption Initiatives

Countries like *Botswana* and *Ghana* have established independent anti-corruption agencies to monitor government spending and investigate misconduct. These initiatives build trust and deter capital misappropriation.

2. Civil Society Engagement

Civil society plays a key role in exposing corruption and advocating for transparency. Governments must protect journalists, activists, and watchdog organizations that hold institutions accountable and raise public awareness.

3. Promoting Ethical Business Practices

African businesses must lead by example, adopting ethical standards that prioritize fair

Chapter 9

competition and discourage exploitative practices. Business associations can help set norms that align profit-making with local reinvestment and long-term development.

Conclusion: Retaining Africa's Wealth for Future Growth

Curbing capital escape is not just an economic necessity—it is a moral imperative. Retaining wealth within African economies ensures that development is driven from within and that prosperity is accessible to all.

By strengthening institutions, embracing tax transparency, investing in digital solutions, and fostering a culture of accountability, African nations can reclaim the resources needed for sustainable progress. This will reduce dependency, encourage innovation, and finance the next generation of leaders, builders, and changemakers.

While the challenge is complex, it is not insurmountable. Through visionary leadership, collective action, and structural reform, Africa can

Generational Shift

break the cycle of capital flight and build a future rooted in equity, empowerment, and resilience—for this generation and the next.

Chapter 10:
Building a Culture of Innovation and Entrepreneurship

Introduction

Innovation and entrepreneurship are the driving forces behind economic growth and social transformation. For Africa to realize its potential as a global economic powerhouse, it must cultivate an environment that supports creativity, risk-taking, and the development of sustainable business ventures.

> "For Africa to realize its potential as a global economic powerhouse, it must cultivate an environment that encourages creativity, risk-taking, and sustainable business ventures."

This chapter explores the critical role innovation and entrepreneurship play in Africa's transformation, examines the challenges African entrepreneurs face, and offers strategies to foster a thriving entrepreneurial ecosystem capable of reshaping the continent's economic landscape.

Understanding the Role of Innovation and Entrepreneurship in Development

Innovation and entrepreneurship drive development by creating jobs, improving productivity, and generating wealth. In the African context, they also provide powerful tools to address deeply rooted challenges—such as access to healthcare, quality education, food security, and clean energy.

Entrepreneurship is not just about launching businesses. It is a mindset—defined by adaptability, creativity, resilience, and a relentless focus on problem-solving. These traits are essential in navigating Africa's dynamic and often unpredictable socioeconomic landscape.

A thriving culture of innovation supports Africa's development goals by:

Chapter 10

1. Creating Jobs and Generating Wealth

Startups and small enterprises are vital job creators, especially in emerging economies. Fostering entrepreneurship allows African nations to tap into their vast youth population, creating employment opportunities, reducing poverty, and stimulating economic activity at the local level.

2. Encouraging Self-Reliance and Reducing Dependence on Foreign Aid

Innovation enables Africans to craft homegrown solutions to their own challenges—moving away from reliance on imported systems or external assistance. Africa should not only consume global ideas but export its own solutions and perspectives.

A shift toward self-reliance strengthens local economies and fuels a renewed sense of pride, ownership, and belief in African capabilities.

3. **Tackling Pressing Challenges with African-Centric Solutions**

Africa's complex challenges require solutions that are relevant, scalable, and culturally grounded. Innovation empowers local communities to build tools that address real needs—from sustainable farming techniques to low-cost medical diagnostics.

4. **Harnessing Local Insight for Global Impact**

Africans are uniquely positioned to understand the intricacies of the challenges facing their communities—from education and healthcare to climate change and political reform. Because these challenges are deeply tied to Africa's cultural heritage, geographical diversity, and social structures, solutions from within are more likely to be sustainable and effective.

These African-led innovations not only address root causes but can also serve as blueprints for similar regions around the world. For example, Kenya's M-Pesa revolutionized mobile banking and inspired financial inclusion

Chapter 10

initiatives globally. Similarly, community-driven healthcare models in rural Africa are being studied and adapted internationally.

When Africa invests in its own ingenuity, it not only meets its own development goals—it contributes to global progress by exporting tested, culturally relevant solutions rooted in resilience and innovation.

> "As Africa continues to embrace homegrown strategies, it not only fosters self-reliance but also positions itself as a contributor to global knowledge and development – exporting practical, tested solutions rooted in African ingenuity and resilience."

Challenges Facing African Innovators and Entrepreneurs

Despite the potential, African entrepreneurs face significant hurdles that stifle innovation and business development. Overcoming these obstacles is crucial to unleashing the continent's creative and economic potential.

1. Limited Access to Funding

Securing capital remains one of the biggest challenges for African entrepreneurs, especially at the startup stage. Traditional banks are risk-averse, often requiring substantial collateral, and tend to favor large, established businesses.

Meanwhile, venture capital and angel investor ecosystems are underdeveloped across much of the continent, leaving early-stage innovators without the resources to scale their ideas.

2. Lack of Supportive Infrastructure

Inconsistent electricity, poor internet access, and inadequate transportation networks raise the cost of doing business and discourage investment. These infrastructure issues hinder productivity and make it harder for small businesses to compete or grow.

Chapter 10

3. Inadequate Education and Skills Development

Many African education systems prioritize rote memorization over critical thinking, creativity, or real-world problem-solving. As a result, many young people lack essential entrepreneurial skills—such as financial literacy, digital competency, and business management.

This disconnect between education and market needs leaves aspiring entrepreneurs underprepared to navigate complex business environments.

4. Restrictive Regulatory Environments

Bureaucratic hurdles make it difficult to launch and sustain a business. High registration costs, inconsistent licensing, and unclear tax policies discourage entrepreneurs and stifle innovation. Simplified and transparent business environments are critical to supporting emerging ventures.

5. Cultural Perceptions of Failure

In many African societies, failure carries a strong stigma. This fear of failure prevents many from experimenting or taking calculated risks—two essential components of innovation. Cultivating a mindset that views failure as a learning process is crucial to fostering a culture of bold ideas and entrepreneurial resilience.

Strategies for Building a Culture of Innovation and Entrepreneurship

To cultivate a thriving culture of innovation and entrepreneurship, African nations must adopt multifaceted strategies that remove systemic barriers and empower individuals with the mindset, tools, and support they need to succeed.

1. **Establishing Access to Funding and Financial Support**

Governments and private sector partners can collaborate to develop funding programs tailored specifically to startups and small enterprises. Tools such as seed funds, microfinancing, and low-interest loans provide essential capital for early-stage entrepreneurs.

Example: *Nigeria's Bank of Industry* has implemented several loan and grant programs

Chapter 10

targeted at young entrepreneurs—especially in agriculture and manufacturing. These initiatives have helped launch thousands of small businesses and stimulated job creation and local economic growth.

2. Investing in Entrepreneurship Education and Skill Development

Educational systems must be restructured to prioritize critical thinking, creativity, and practical skills. Schools and universities can integrate entrepreneurship courses, digital literacy programs, and business competitions to inspire students to view innovation as a viable path.

Example: *Strathmore Business School in Kenya* runs programs that introduce entrepreneurship education at the primary and secondary school levels—teaching students business basics and financial literacy from an early age.

3. **Building Supportive Ecosystems through Innovation Hubs and Incubators**

Incubators, accelerators, and innovation hubs provide mentorship, business training, and access to investor networks. These platforms foster collaboration, reduce isolation among entrepreneurs, and offer the infrastructure needed to bring ideas to life.

Example: *MEST Africa*, a pan-African incubator, offers training in software development, business strategy, and market analysis. Its graduates have gone on to launch successful startups in fintech, healthcare, and e-commerce—showcasing the continent's capacity for innovation.

4. **Reforming Regulatory Environments to Reduce Barriers**

Governments can spur innovation by making business processes simpler, more affordable, and more transparent. Streamlining registration, reducing bureaucratic bottlenecks, and

Chapter 10

implementing favorable tax policies help foster a startup-friendly environment.

Example: *Rwanda* allows entrepreneurs to register a business in under six hours, making it one of the most efficient systems in the world. This reform has triggered a surge in SME growth and helped position Rwanda as a regional hub for business.

5. Encouraging a Cultural Shift Toward Risk-taking and Innovation

To build a truly entrepreneurial society, cultural attitudes toward failure must change. Public campaigns, education, and storytelling can reshape perceptions of failure—reframing it as part of the learning process rather than something to be feared or avoided.

Celebrating entrepreneurial success stories and normalizing setbacks fosters a climate where experimentation and bold thinking are encouraged.

6. Teaching Persistence in the Face of Failure

Persistence is a defining trait of transformative leaders. History offers powerful lessons:

Abraham Lincoln faced repeated personal losses and electoral defeats, yet famously said,

"My great concern is not whether you have failed, but whether you are content with your failure."

His journey underscores that failure is not an endpoint—it's part of the path to impact.

Thomas Edison, after thousands of failed attempts to invent the light bulb, remarked,

"I have not failed. I've just found 10,000 ways that won't work." This mindset—viewing failure as feedback—remains foundational for any innovator.

These examples remind us that success often lies on the other side of persistence. A resilient mindset can turn repeated setbacks into the building blocks of breakthrough innovation.

Chapter 10

7. Learning from Lessons in Endurance and Dedication

Few stories exemplify enduring commitment to change better than **Nelson Mandela**. Despite enduring 27 years in prison, he emerged not with vengeance, but with vision—determined to unify a divided South Africa.

Mandela once said:

"I have walked that long road to freedom. I have tried not to falter... But I have discovered the secret that after climbing a great hill, one only finds that there are many more hills to climb." This resilience, rooted in love for his people and continent, serves as a call to today's youth: keep climbing. Keep striving for a better Africa.

Likewise, Jerry Rawlings of Ghana demonstrated bold leadership grounded in accountability and national pride. He emphasized that building a self-reliant Africa required integrity, courage, and commitment to future generations.

Rawlings once said:

"We must create an Africa that is strong and able to bequeath a legacy of self-worth, self-dignity, and national pride to future generations."

These African leaders embody the spirit of perseverance—not for personal glory, but for the continent's long-term transformation. Their stories serve as guideposts for a new generation of innovators and changemakers.

Spotlight on Africa's Emerging Innovators

Across the continent, young African entrepreneurs are pioneering solutions to some of their communities' most urgent challenges. Their journeys reveal the powerful impact of a culture that supports innovation, risk-taking, and creative thinking.

1. Technology and Digital Innovation

In regions with limited access to traditional banking, African entrepreneurs have used technology to bridge the gap. Kenya's *M-Pesa* mobile payment system has revolutionized financial access for millions, becoming a global model for mobile money. Health-tech, e-commerce, and logistics platforms are further proof of how digital innovation can improve lives and expand economic opportunity.

2. Sustainable Agriculture

Agriculture remains central to African livelihoods, and young innovators are applying agri-tech tools, sustainable practices, and new financing models to transform the sector.

Example: *Farmcrowdy*, a Nigerian startup, allows everyday citizens to sponsor farms, providing capital to local farmers while delivering profits to investors. This model supports food security while creating economic inclusion.

3. Renewable Energy

With unreliable access to electricity in many regions, renewable energy startups are offering sustainable alternatives.

Example: *Lumos* in Nigeria and *M-KOPA* in East Africa are delivering affordable, solar-powered energy systems to off-grid households and small businesses—expanding access and boosting productivity across rural communities.

4. Health and Education

Ed-tech and health-tech are bridging service gaps, especially in rural and underserved areas.

Example: *LifeBank*, a Nigerian startup, uses technology to deliver critical medical supplies like blood and oxygen to hospitals—saving lives by solving last-mile delivery challenges.

Example: In Kenya, *Eneza Education* provides affordable e-learning content via mobile phones, helping students in remote areas access quality education and bridge the rural-urban learning gap.

Conclusion: Paving the Way for a Thriving, Innovative Africa

Creating a culture of innovation and entrepreneurship is essential for Africa to break free from cycles of dependency and realize its potential. By promoting creativity, risk-taking, and resilience, African nations can build an ecosystem

Chapter 10

that supports the next generation of changemakers and problem-solvers.

Governments, educators, businesses, and civil society all have a role to play in nurturing this ecosystem. By investing in homegrown solutions and celebrating innovators, Africa can become not just a consumer of global ideas, but a producer and exporter of transformative innovations.

Ultimately, this journey is about empowering people to recognize opportunity where others see obstacles. As Africa's spirit of innovation grows, it will not only change lives locally—it will redefine the continent's global influence.

A Story of Liberian Entrepreneurship

In the early 1990s, Liberia was plunged into a brutal civil war, displacing nearly everyone in the country. Many Liberians fled to neighboring nations as refugees, while others sought safety in remote areas within Liberia. Among them was Floyd, a young man fresh out of high school who had just begun his journey in life as a street vendor,

Generational Shift

moving his small market on wheels around town. Floyd brought his business directly to the people. While his trade provided just enough to cover his basic needs—food, shelter, and clothing—he gained valuable business experience.

But when war erupted, Floyd, like countless others, was forced to abandon his familiar life, retreating to a small, remote village for safety.

Days dragged on in the secluded village with limited options to escape or rebuild. One day, while fishing in a nearby creek, Floyd noticed shimmering rocks along the creek's edge. His curiosity grew—could these shining stones hint at something more valuable beneath? Inspired by childhood tales of gold and diamonds, Floyd gathered a few companions and began digging. To their amazement, they uncovered gold.

In the midst of poverty and displacement, Floyd had found wealth. He soon employed villagers to help him dig, and when he amassed enough gold, he took the risk of traveling to neighboring countries like Ivory Coast and Guinea to sell it. Encouraged by these sales, Floyd

Chapter 10

expanded his operations, buying gold from others and scaling up to meet growing demand. Even with limited resources and constant danger, Floyd was relentless. He understood that he was sitting on a wealth of opportunities—just as Africa is today.

Floyd's story is a powerful reminder to Africans of the vast opportunities surrounding them, waiting to be harnessed. Despite his challenging circumstances, Floyd used his entrepreneurial spirit to create wealth not only for himself but for his entire community. Africa, like Floyd, sits on untapped potential—whether in natural resources, agriculture, technology, or real estate. By pursuing entrepreneurship, Africans can build wealth, create jobs, and strengthen their economies.

Floyd's rise from street vendor to multimillionaire underscores a key message: Africa doesn't need to look outside for wealth. The continent holds immense riches and opportunities within its borders. With persistence and a willingness to take risks, Africans can shape a prosperous future—where wealth is generated by Africans, for Africans, and strengthens the entire continent.

After the war quieted down in the late 1990s and early 2000s, Floyd started a company called Jungle Water Group of Investment (JWGI). Today, Jungle Water Group of Investment is worth millions of dollars. Floyd has diversified into real estate and now owns some of the finest hotels in Liberia. Jungle Water Group has also built private electrical grids and supplies purified drinking water.

Floyd is a Liberian who has never lived outside his country. He is one of Liberia's wealthiest individuals, providing jobs for hundreds of Liberians.

His journey reflects the story of Africa itself—a continent sitting on immense wealth and opportunity that others have long exploited. But with vision and determination, that narrative can change.

Chapter 11:
Women as Pioneers of Change in African Societies

Introduction

Across Africa, women have long played powerful, though often overlooked, roles in shaping society. From leading grassroots movements to advocating political reform, African women have consistently challenged norms, defended their rights, and blazed pathways for change.

This chapter explores the pivotal role women play in Africa's ongoing evolution—highlighting the barriers they face and the transformative impact of empowering women to lead.

The Legacy of Women Leaders in African History

Africa's history is rich with examples of visionary women leaders. Yet, their stories are too often minimized or overshadowed.

Generational Shift

Figures like Queen Nzinga of Angola, who led resistance against colonial forces, and Yaa Asantewaa of the Ashanti Empire, who rallied her people against British invaders, stand as enduring symbols of strength and leadership in the face of oppression.

In modern history, women like Wangari Maathai, the Kenyan Nobel Peace Prize winner and environmentalist, and Ellen Johnson Sirleaf, Africa's first female president, have continued this legacy. Sirleaf's leadership in Liberia during and after civil war showed the profound impact of women in governance and post-conflict reconstruction.

> "From championing political reform to leading grassroots movements, African women have been pivotal in challenging societal norms, advocating for rights, and creating pathways for change."

These trailblazers—and many others—are woven into the fabric of Africa's political and social history. Their stories inspire a new

Chapter 11

generation of women across the continent who are rising as entrepreneurs, activists, politicians, and thought leaders.

Barriers to Women's Advancement in African Societies

While progress has been made, significant obstacles continue to limit women's full participation in African society. Understanding and addressing these barriers is critical to unlocking the continent's potential.

1. Gender Discrimination and Cultural Norms

Patriarchal values remain deeply rooted in many African cultures. Women are often expected to prioritize domestic and caregiving roles, which restricts their participation in public life, particularly in leadership, politics, and business.

These cultural norms reinforce gender inequality and discourage women from pursuing personal ambitions or leadership opportunities.

2. Lack of Access to Education

Education is a powerful tool for empowerment, yet many African girls face serious barriers. Early marriage, poverty, and family expectations often prevent girls from attending or completing school. This lack of education limits their future opportunities and perpetuates intergenerational cycles of poverty and dependency.

3. Economic Inequality and Limited Access to Resources

Women frequently face limited access to land, credit, and financial capital. In many countries, customary laws and discriminatory inheritance practices deny women property rights. Without resources, women struggle to start businesses, invest in their families, or gain economic independence.

4. Underrepresentation in Leadership and Decision-making

Though women make up half the population, they remain underrepresented in political office, corporate leadership, and policymaking spaces.

Chapter 11

This imbalance means that critical issues affecting women—such as health, education, and social protection—often lack the advocacy and policy attention they deserve.

5. Gender-Based Violence (GBV)

GBV remains a pervasive challenge across the continent, affecting women of all ages. Beyond the physical and emotional harm, violence against women reinforces systemic power imbalances and severely limits their ability to participate freely in social, economic, and political life.

Empowering Women as Catalysts for Societal Transformation

Empowering women and addressing systemic gender barriers is not only a matter of justice—it is a powerful engine for societal transformation. When women are empowered, they uplift families, strengthen communities, and contribute to healthier, more resilient, and prosperous societies.

Here are key strategies for empowering African women and unlocking their transformative potential:

1. Expanding Access to Education and Skills Development

Education remains one of the most effective tools for breaking cycles of poverty and inequality. When girls and women are educated, they gain the knowledge, confidence, and skills needed to pursue opportunities, increase their income, and contribute meaningfully to their societies.

Example: *Rwanda* has made substantial investments in girls' education, resulting in one of the highest female enrollment rates in Africa. This commitment has not only improved outcomes for women but also contributed to Rwanda's overall economic growth and social stability.

2. Economic Empowerment through Microlending and Entrepreneurship

Access to microfinance, capital, and business training enables women to start and grow their own enterprises—boosting both household income and community development. Supporting women economically increases their

Chapter 11

independence and influence in decision-making at home and in society.

Example: In *Kenya*, the **Table Banking** model empowers women by allowing them to pool savings, offer small loans to one another, and fund personal or business ventures. This grassroots initiative has enhanced financial inclusion and created economic security for thousands of women across the country.

3. Increasing Women's Representation in Leadership

Representation matters. When women hold seats at the decision-making table—whether in government, corporate leadership, or community councils—they bring diverse perspectives and champion issues often overlooked in male-dominated spaces, including maternal health, child welfare, and education.

Example: *Senegal* passed a gender parity law requiring political parties to have at least 50% women on their electoral lists. This has significantly increased women's presence in parliament and influenced the creation of policies centered on family welfare and gender equity.

4. Addressing Gender-Based Violence through Policy and Education

To create environments where women can thrive, countries must combat gender-based violence (GBV) through stronger legal protections, survivor support services, and public education that challenges harmful gender norms.

Example: *South Africa's Thuthuzela Care Centres* provide comprehensive care to survivors of GBV—including medical, legal, and psychosocial support. These centers are part of a national strategy to support survivors and reduce secondary trauma, offering a holistic model that can be replicated elsewhere.

5. Fostering Women's Networks and Mentorship Programs

Mentorship and networking opportunities help women share knowledge, build confidence, and overcome systemic barriers together. These programs foster solidarity and equip women with

Chapter 11

the skills and connections needed to thrive in leadership, business, and community development.

Example: The African Women in Business Initiative (AWIB) provides female entrepreneurs with training, mentorship, and opportunities to advocate for inclusive economic policies. The network has empowered women across the continent to launch ventures, scale businesses, and lead change within their sectors.

Spotlight on African Women Pioneers Driving Change

Across Africa, women are leading transformative movements that address some of the continent's most urgent challenges—from education and healthcare to technology, agriculture, and sustainability. Their stories exemplify the powerful role empowered women play in building stronger, more equitable societies.

1. Health and Social Justice Advocates

African women are at the forefront of improving public health and advancing social justice. **Dr.**

Agnes Binagwaho, Rwanda's former Minister of Health, is one such leader. Her policies and programs significantly reduced maternal and infant mortality rates, expanding healthcare access and strengthening Rwanda's health infrastructure. Her legacy underscores how women in leadership roles can drive meaningful, systemic change in public health.

2. Entrepreneurs in Technology and Innovation

African women are also breaking barriers in the technology sector, developing innovative solutions tailored to local needs. **Rebecca Enonchong**, founder of *AppsTech* in Cameroon, is a trailblazer in African tech entrepreneurship. Her work has not only reshaped the tech landscape in Africa but also inspired countless women to pursue careers in STEM, transforming the narrative around women in innovation.

Chapter 11

3. Environmental and Agricultural Leaders

Women have long played a key role in environmental advocacy and sustainable agriculture.

Wangari Maathai, the late Kenyan Nobel laureate, led the *Green Belt Movement*, which empowered women to plant millions of trees, combat deforestation, and promote environmental stewardship. Her work illustrates how women's leadership in environmental sustainability fosters both ecological and social resilience.

4. Educators and Advocates for Girls' Rights

Education remains a cornerstone of gender equity. Women leaders and advocates have fought tirelessly to ensure that girls receive access to quality education.

Initiatives by global figures like **Malala Yousafzai**, alongside organizations such as *CAMFED* (Campaign for Female Education), founded by **Ann Cotton**, have removed barriers to education for girls in Africa. Their efforts have helped thousands of girls go to school, unlocking future opportunities and shifting cultural attitudes toward female education.

Conclusion: Paving the Way for Inclusive Growth and Empowerment

African women are not just participants in the continent's development—they are leading it. Their leadership creates ripple effects across communities, economies, and generations. Empowering women is not a singular achievement; it is a catalyst for inclusive growth, sustainable development, and societal resilience.

Africa's future depends on fully embracing women as leaders, innovators, educators, and changemakers. By breaking down systemic barriers, nurturing leadership, and investing in girls and women, African societies can harness a vast reservoir of untapped talent and vision.

As the continent continues to evolve, the role of women will remain central to building a more equitable, dynamic, and prosperous Africa—one shaped by the hands and hearts of those who have always been vital to its progress.

Chapter 12:
Environmental Stewardship and Sustainable Development

Introduction

Africa's future prosperity is closely tied to its natural wealth—from fertile soils and diverse ecosystems to mineral reserves and renewable energy potential. However, the continent also faces escalating environmental challenges: climate change, deforestation, water scarcity, and biodiversity loss. Addressing these issues is no longer optional—it is essential.

Sustainable development—growth that meets present needs without compromising the needs of future generations—demands a clear focus on environmental stewardship. This chapter explores Africa's environmental landscape, examines key challenges, and highlights community-driven solutions that point the way toward a sustainable future.

Africa's Environmental Landscape and Key Challenges

Africa is one of the world's most biodiverse regions, home to iconic wildlife, rich ecosystems, and landscapes vital to global environmental health. Yet these natural assets are under increasing threat. Left unaddressed, these issues will compromise the continent's economy, public health, and food systems.

1. Climate Change and Its Impact

Despite contributing relatively little to global greenhouse gas emissions, Africa is experiencing some of the most severe effects of climate change. Rising temperatures, erratic rainfall, droughts, floods, and storms are disrupting agriculture, diminishing water availability, and displacing communities—especially in coastal and low-lying regions.

These changes are accelerating food insecurity and threatening livelihoods across both urban and rural areas. From the Horn of Africa to Southern Africa, unpredictable climate patterns

Chapter 12

are placing immense strain on water and food systems.

2. Deforestation and Desertification

Expanding agriculture, logging, and urban growth are driving widespread deforestation. This not only releases stored carbon but also destroys habitats, reduces rainfall, and depletes soil quality—undermining long-term food production.

Desertification is another escalating issue, particularly in the Sahel region, where the Sahara continues to expand southward. As arable land diminishes, rural communities face increased poverty, forced migration, and conflict over scarce resources.

3. Loss of Biodiversity

Africa's rich biodiversity—essential to its ecological balance and cultural identity—is being lost at an alarming rate. Habitat destruction, illegal wildlife trade, and climate change are reducing species populations and degrading ecosystems.

This loss impacts everything from food production to tourism and even medicine. When biodiversity declines, ecosystems lose their ability to adapt to stress, making them more vulnerable to disease, degradation, and climate extremes.

4. Water Scarcity and Pollution

Access to safe and clean water is becoming increasingly scarce due to population growth, urbanization, and climate variability. At the same time, industrial waste, agricultural runoff, and inadequate sanitation systems are polluting vital water sources.

Urban centers like Lagos, Kinshasa, Accra, and Monrovia are especially affected. Many residents rely on open drainage systems and untreated surface water, exposing millions to diseases like cholera, typhoid, and hepatitis. In informal settlements, the absence of toilets or waste treatment options exacerbates public health risks.

Solutions:

To address these challenges, governments and communities can adopt decentralized water treatment and sanitation solutions. Low-cost, eco-friendly systems such as bio-digesters and composting toilets offer viable alternatives in dense urban environments. Public education campaigns can further promote hygienic practices, while public-private partnerships can mobilize investment in sanitation infrastructure. Together, these approaches can improve health, protect ecosystems, and make African cities more resilient.

5. Waste Management and Plastic Pollution

Rapid urban growth has outpaced infrastructure development, leading to widespread mismanagement of solid waste. Streets, waterways, and drainage systems in many African cities are clogged with plastic and non-biodegradable waste, contributing to urban flooding, ecosystem damage, and health hazards.

Without formal recycling systems or landfill regulation, plastic waste is often burned or dumped, polluting the air and soil. Marine and river ecosystems are also suffering, with plastics harming fish, birds, and aquatic habitats vital to food security and biodiversity.

The Importance of Sustainable Development for Africa

Sustainable development offers a pathway for Africa to address its environmental challenges while promoting inclusive economic growth, social equity, and long-term resilience. By aligning environmental protection with development goals, African nations can foster prosperity while safeguarding the well-being of current and future generations.

> "Africa is one of the most biodiverse regions in the world, home to unique ecosystems, wildlife, and landscapes that are invaluable to the planet's health and humanity's heritage."

1. **Securing Food and Water Resources**

Sustainable agricultural practices and smart water management are critical for food security. Techniques such as agroforestry, rainwater harvesting, and drip irrigation help conserve natural resources, improve yields, and ensure access to clean water—especially in regions affected by climate change and soil degradation.

2. Reducing Vulnerability to Climate Change

By building climate resilience, African countries can reduce the risks posed by droughts, floods, and extreme weather events. Initiatives like wetland restoration, mangrove protection, and improved urban planning help buffer communities against environmental shocks while strengthening ecosystems.

3. Supporting Economic Growth through Green Jobs

Sustainable sectors—such as renewable energy, eco-tourism, and regenerative agriculture—offer economic growth opportunities without sacrificing environmental integrity. These industries generate green jobs that support livelihoods while fostering environmental stewardship.

4. Fostering Healthier Living Environments

Sustainable development improves public health by reducing exposure to pollution, improving sanitation, and securing access to clean air and water. Healthier environments mean fewer disease outbreaks, stronger communities, and reduced burdens on healthcare systems.

African-led Solutions to Environmental Challenges

African communities, innovators, and leaders are creating homegrown solutions that reflect local knowledge, resilience, and creativity. These initiatives offer scalable models for sustainable development, environmental restoration, and economic inclusion.

1. Agroforestry and Regenerative Agriculture

In regions grappling with land degradation and food insecurity, agroforestry—planting trees alongside crops—and regenerative farming techniques restore soil fertility, reduce erosion, and enhance biodiversity.

Example: *The Great Green Wall* is a bold initiative spanning across the **Sahel region**, aiming to halt the spread of the Sahara by cultivating a mosaic of green spaces. Driven by community participation, the project not only combats desertification but also creates jobs and revives rural economies.

2. Renewable Energy and Off-grid Solutions

Africa's solar and wind potential can power the continent sustainably, especially in rural areas where grid infrastructure is limited.

Example: *M-KOPA Solar* in **Kenya** provides affordable, off-grid solar systems to millions of households. These systems support lighting, cooking, and communication—improving quality of life while reducing dependence on polluting fuels like kerosene and charcoal.

3. Conservation and Eco-tourism

Community-based conservation protects wildlife, preserves biodiversity, and creates income through eco-tourism.

Example: *Botswana* has pioneered **community-run wildlife conservancies**, where tourism revenue directly benefits local populations. This model has led to successful conservation outcomes while promoting economic opportunity and environmental awareness.

4. Water Conservation and Efficient Irrigation

Innovative water-saving practices help ensure long-term agricultural productivity and water availability.

Example: In **Ethiopia**, smallholder farmers are using **drip irrigation systems** to maximize water efficiency and improve yields. These low-tech, high-impact systems are critical in water-scarce regions and demonstrate scalable sustainability.

5. Waste Management Innovations

Rapid urbanization requires creative solutions for waste and plastic pollution.

Example: *Trashy Bags Africa* in **Ghana** collects plastic waste and transforms it into reusable bags and accessories. This initiative reduces environmental pollution, provides employment, and promotes a circular economy mindset.

Chapter 12

The Role of Youth and Community in Environmental Stewardship

Africa's youth and communities are central to building a culture of environmental stewardship. Across the continent, young people and grassroots organizations are taking action—raising awareness, driving behavioral change, and leading sustainable initiatives. Their engagement is not only a symbol of hope but a vital force for lasting environmental impact.

1. Youth-led Environmental Movements

Young Africans are increasingly stepping into leadership roles in the fight against climate change. Through advocacy, protests, and social media campaigns, they are pushing for climate justice, demanding policy reform, and mobilizing communities.

Example: *Vanessa Nakate*, a Ugandan climate activist, has emerged as a powerful voice on the global stage. Her advocacy highlights the disproportionate impact of climate change on African communities and amplifies the voices of underrepresented youth in international climate conversations.

2. Community-based Conservation and Resource Management

When communities are empowered to manage natural resources, environmental stewardship becomes a shared responsibility. Community-led conservation programs often blend traditional knowledge with sustainable practices, creating effective, culturally rooted solutions.

Example: In *Enduimet, Tanzania*, local communities manage wildlife corridors and conservation areas. Their efforts have improved biodiversity protection while generating income through eco-tourism, proving that community ownership fosters environmental and economic resilience.

3. Environmental Education and Awareness

Education is a cornerstone of sustainability. Programs that engage students and communities in environmental issues build awareness and inspire long-term change. Environmental

Chapter 12

education encourages responsible choices and fosters a lifelong ethic of stewardship.

Example: *Green Fingers Initiative* in **Nigeria** teaches children about sustainability through activities like tree planting, waste management, and eco-gardening. These early lessons help shape a generation that values and protects the environment.

Policy Recommendations for Sustainable Development

To build a sustainable future, African governments must implement forward-thinking policies that balance growth with environmental responsibility. Key policy priorities include:

1. Incentivizing Renewable Energy

Provide tax breaks, subsidies, and investment incentives for solar, wind, and other renewable energy sources. Support private sector participation and expand off-grid solutions to increase energy access.

2. Implementing Sustainable Land Use and Forestry Policies

Develop land management frameworks that prevent deforestation, promote reforestation, and encourage sustainable farming. Prioritize agroforestry and soil conservation to safeguard ecosystems and ensure food security.

3. Enforcing Waste Management Regulations

Strengthen waste management systems through legislation and public-private partnerships. Promote recycling, reduce single-use plastics, and invest in waste processing infrastructure to reduce environmental and health risks.

4. Supporting Conservation and Protected Areas

Expand and enforce protected areas while involving communities in their management. Promote eco-tourism and biodiversity conservation through incentives, education, and legal protections.

5. Adapting to Climate Change

Develop and implement national adaptation plans that address vulnerability hotspots. Invest in early warning systems, disaster-resilient infrastructure, and public education to reduce risk and build resilience.

Conclusion: Building a Sustainable Future for Africa

Africa's future depends on its ability to protect and preserve its natural resources. Environmental stewardship is no longer a choice—it is a necessity. By embracing sustainable development, African nations can unlock long-term prosperity while ensuring that future generations inherit a healthy, thriving continent.

The solutions are already emerging—from local innovators to youth-led movements to community-based programs. By scaling these efforts and implementing supportive policies, Africa can become a global leader in sustainability.

A greener, more resilient Africa is not only possible—it is within reach. With commitment,

Generational Shift

collaboration, and courage, the continent can chart a future that honors its heritage, uplifts its people, and safeguards the planet.

Chapter 13:
The Effects of Trade Deficits on the African Economy

Trade deficits—when a country imports more than it exports—remain a persistent economic challenge for many African nations. While international trade is essential for economic growth, the structure of trade in much of Africa has led to imbalances. Many countries rely heavily on the importation of finished goods, from consumer products to industrial equipment, while primarily exporting raw materials. This model creates a dependency on external markets and leaves local economies vulnerable to global price fluctuations.

Over time, consistent trade deficits deplete foreign currency reserves, weaken national currencies, and contribute to inflation—reducing citizens' purchasing power and increasing the cost of living. Moreover, countries often resort to external borrowing to finance their trade gaps,

Generational Shift

leading to rising national debt and long-term financial instability.

To address these issues, African countries must shift from being consumers of imported goods to becoming producers and exporters of value-added products. Investing in local manufacturing, agro-processing, and other productive sectors is critical to reducing import reliance and strengthening economic sovereignty. Support for small and medium-sized enterprises (SMEs), particularly in industries like agriculture, textiles, and construction materials, is also key to building a sustainable and balanced trade environment.

Regional frameworks like the **African Continental Free Trade Area (AfCFTA)** present additional opportunities. By strengthening intra-African trade, countries can reduce dependence on overseas markets, diversify their trade portfolios, and stimulate homegrown industries. Taken together, these steps can help transition African economies toward trade surplus models that promote long-term stability and self-reliance.

Chapter 13

Examples of African Countries Reducing Trade Deficits

1. Ethiopia: Advancing Manufacturing and Export Capacity

Ethiopia has made notable strides in narrowing its trade deficit by investing in local manufacturing, particularly in the textile and leather sectors. The development of industrial parks, such as **Hawassa Industrial Park**, has attracted global companies to manufacture goods within the country. By producing apparel and footwear locally, Ethiopia not only reduces import dependence but also generates export revenues, creates jobs, and moves up the value chain.

2. Rwanda: Promoting Local Production through 'Made in Rwanda'

Rwanda's **Made in Rwanda** initiative encourages domestic manufacturing across key sectors like fashion, electronics, and building materials. This policy has fueled local entrepreneurship, cut reliance on imported goods, and retained economic value within national borders.

Additionally, Rwanda's emphasis on processing high-value exports such as tea and coffee, rather than exporting them raw, enhances export earnings and diversifies the economy.

3. Nigeria: Diversification Beyond Oil

Nigeria, long reliant on oil exports, has launched several initiatives to diversify its economy. The **Economic Recovery and Growth Plan (ERGP)** supports investments in agriculture, technology, and manufacturing. Local rice production has expanded significantly, thanks to Central Bank-backed programs, reducing the need for rice imports and improving food security. These steps

> "While international trade is vital for economic growth, African countries often rely heavily on importing finished goods while exporting primarily raw materials, leading to trade imbalances that strain local economies."

are gradually lowering Nigeria's trade deficit while making the economy more resilient.

Chapter 13

4. Kenya: Industrialization Through the Big Four Agenda

Kenya's **Big Four Agenda** prioritizes manufacturing as a pillar of national development. Focused efforts in food processing and pharmaceuticals have expanded domestic production and job creation. By increasing exports of processed agricultural products and reducing reliance on imported consumer goods, Kenya is working toward a more balanced trade profile and sustainable industrial growth.

5. Ghana: One District, One Factory Initiative

Ghana's **One District, One Factory** initiative supports the creation of small-scale industrial plants in each district. This grassroots industrial policy boosts local manufacturing and reduces import dependency. The government's focus on agro-processing—particularly in value-added cocoa exports—has helped retain more revenue domestically, stimulated job creation, and gradually improved the national trade balance.

Conclusion: Toward Trade Resilience and Economic Independence

Trade deficits need not be permanent fixtures of African economies. The success stories of Ethiopia, Rwanda, Nigeria, Kenya, and Ghana show that strategic investments in domestic industries, value addition, and regional trade can reverse trade imbalances and foster economic resilience.

As more nations adopt these models — tailored to their unique resources and challenges — Africa can shift toward a future of trade self-sufficiency, export diversification, and greater control over its economic destiny.

Chapter 14:
Opportunity Economies for Greater Human Flourishing

Opportunity economies are designed to ensure that every individual—regardless of background—has equitable access to the resources, training, and support needed to pursue personal goals and contribute meaningfully to society. For Africa, the creation of such economies is not merely an economic imperative but a moral and social one. It involves transforming the continent's development agenda from one focused solely on GDP growth to one centered on maximizing human potential.

In an opportunity economy, success is not limited to a privileged few. Instead, systems and policies are intentionally structured to eliminate systemic barriers, expand access to education and healthcare, and foster environments where innovation and entrepreneurship can thrive. This people-first approach prioritizes inclusivity, dignity, and self-actualization, creating a foundation for sustainable growth and resilient communities.

Laying the Foundations of Opportunity

Building opportunity economies in Africa requires a comprehensive, multi-sectoral strategy that integrates social development with economic planning. This includes:

1. Access to Quality Education

Education remains the cornerstone of any opportunity economy. African governments must invest in accessible, high-quality education systems that emphasize not only academic achievement but also critical thinking, creativity, and technical skills. Vocational training and entrepreneurship education are essential to prepare youth for a dynamic and competitive global economy.

2. Healthcare for Productivity and Dignity

Without access to basic healthcare, individuals cannot participate fully in society or the economy.

Chapter 14

Opportunity economies must ensure equitable healthcare systems that prioritize preventive care, maternal health, and the treatment of chronic conditions. A healthy population is a productive population—and essential for national development.

3. Inclusive Infrastructure Development

Physical and digital infrastructure are the arteries through which opportunity flows. Roads, transportation, broadband internet, and reliable electricity connect individuals to markets, jobs, and services. By investing in infrastructure that serves both urban and rural communities, governments can bridge opportunity gaps and facilitate inclusive growth.

4. Support for SMEs and Entrepreneurship

Small and medium-sized enterprises (SMEs) are the backbone of most African economies. Policies that support access to finance, reduce regulatory burdens, and provide mentorship and incubation services can empower entrepreneurs to create jobs, drive innovation, and generate wealth from within local communities.

5. Digital Inclusion and Innovation

Technology is a powerful equalizer when paired with access. Digital literacy programs, affordable internet, and investments in local tech ecosystems can help individuals participate in the digital economy, build new platforms, and create scalable solutions to community challenges.

Designing for Equity and Inclusion

Opportunity economies must also be intentionally inclusive. Gender equality, youth engagement, and the empowerment of marginalized communities are non-negotiable components of a sustainable future. Women and young people must be represented in leadership, education, and workforce development efforts.

Additionally, social support programs—such as affordable housing, food security, and mental health services—are essential safety nets that allow individuals to focus on growth rather than survival. These systems help stabilize families

Chapter 14

and communities, ensuring that poverty does not become a permanent barrier to opportunity.

The Outcome: Human Flourishing as the New Metric

The ultimate goal of opportunity economies is not just economic performance but human flourishing. When citizens are given the tools and freedom to realize their full potential, societies become more dynamic, resilient, and innovative. African nations that embrace this model will not only reduce inequality and poverty but will cultivate populations equipped to solve their own problems, build competitive industries, and lead on the global stage.

Opportunity economies are, therefore, not simply a policy aspiration—they are a prerequisite for a prosperous, just, and self-reliant Africa.

Chapter 15:
From Poverty Alleviation to Prosperity: Shifting the Focus to Wealth Creation

For generations, much of Africa's development strategy has centered on poverty alleviation—a necessary yet limited approach to addressing the continent's socioeconomic challenges. While these efforts are essential in providing immediate relief, they tend to focus on survival: securing food, shelter, and basic healthcare. This survival-oriented strategy often reinforces the status quo rather than transforming it.

By contrast, a wealth creation mindset promotes long-term prosperity and sustainable development. It encourages individuals and communities to harness opportunities that generate lasting economic empowerment. This chapter explores the distinction between survival-based development and wealth creation,

Chapter 15

advocating for a mindset shift that goes beyond reducing poverty to actively fostering prosperity and unlocking human potential.

Understanding the Poverty Alleviation Model

Poverty alleviation emerged in response to extreme deprivation, particularly in areas with limited access to services and opportunity. Governments, NGOs, and international organizations have invested heavily in short-term relief through food aid, housing support, microfinance, and social welfare programs. These interventions are vital during crises and in regions of persistent inequality.

However, this model is often reactive and temporary. It focuses on immediate needs—cash transfers, subsidies, and small-scale income projects—designed to lift individuals just above the poverty line. The underlying survival mindset is about securing enough to get by. While crucial, this approach does not lay the foundation for long-term growth or economic self-sufficiency.

The limitations of this model become evident when viewed through a systemic lens. Even when poverty rates decline incrementally, dependency often remains. There is little emphasis on innovation or large-scale entrepreneurship, and the reliance on external aid persists. As a result, local capabilities are underdeveloped, and opportunities for endogenous economic growth are limited.

The Wealth Creation Mindset

In contrast, a wealth creation model shifts the conversation from survival to transformation. It focuses on enabling individuals, communities, and nations to thrive through innovation, investment, entrepreneurship, and education. This mindset encourages people to view challenges as opportunities and to actively build value—economically and socially—for themselves and their communities.

Wealth creation reframes development as empowerment. It's about equipping individuals to build businesses, create jobs, and invest in local

Chapter 15

solutions. The focus moves from consumption and dependency to agency and innovation. People are seen not just as laborers or recipients of aid but as producers, owners, and architects of value.

Here, wealth is not defined solely by money. It includes knowledge, networks, property, and the ability to generate sustainable solutions. Wealth creation strategies foster resilience and opportunity by emphasizing education, access to capital, secure property rights, and the infrastructure necessary for economic participation. While poverty alleviation addresses survival, wealth creation drives transformation—empowering individuals to fulfill their potential and contribute meaningfully to society.

Key Pillars of Wealth Creation

Transitioning from poverty alleviation to wealth creation requires strategic investments in core pillars that enable long-term growth. These include education and skills development, entrepreneurship, access to capital, and inclusive governance.

Generational Shift

1. Education and Skills Development

Education is fundamental to wealth creation. In a survival economy, learning often stops at basic literacy and numeracy. A wealth-focused model calls for education that cultivates critical thinking, problem-solving, and creativity. It demands access to higher education, vocational training, and digital literacy.

Africa's demographic dividend—its large, youthful population—can be harnessed through education that meets market demands. Programs focused on entrepreneurship, STEM fields (science, technology, engineering, mathematics), and technical skills will equip young Africans not just to participate in the global economy, but to shape it.

2. Entrepreneurship and Innovation

Entrepreneurship is the engine of wealth creation. Unlike survival economies, which often discourage risk-taking due to the absence of safety nets, wealth creation economies embrace innovation and calculated risk. Entrepreneurs identify gaps in the market, develop creative solutions, and generate wealth through ventures that create jobs and deliver valuable products and services.

African economies that nurture entrepreneurship are better positioned to reduce unemployment, stimulate local production, and decrease reliance on imported goods. Programs that provide mentorship, training, and networking opportunities can help cultivate this entrepreneurial spirit. Moreover, fostering innovation ecosystems—such as tech hubs, incubators, and accelerators—offers young Africans the space and support to develop ideas into viable businesses.

3. Access to Capital

Wealth creation cannot flourish without access to capital. Entrepreneurs and innovators need financial support to transform their ideas into scalable ventures. Traditional poverty alleviation models often rely on microfinance, offering small loans intended for subsistence-level activity. While useful for basic needs, this approach does not support sustainable business growth.

To truly support wealth creation, African financial systems must expand access to larger pools of funding, including venture capital, equity financing, and SME-focused loans. Governments, private investors, and development banks should work together to create investment-friendly environments and ensure that capital is accessible to entrepreneurs with high-growth potential.

4. Inclusive Governance and Infrastructure

Wealth creation is also tied to inclusive governance and robust infrastructure. Governments must implement policies that ensure equitable access to resources, protect property rights, and maintain political stability. At the same time, infrastructure development—such as reliable energy, transportation networks, and digital connectivity—is essential for enabling businesses to thrive and access broader markets.

Countries that invest in infrastructure make it easier for entrepreneurs to operate efficiently

Chapter 15

and expand. Roads, ports, and broadband reduce costs, boost productivity, and encourage regional trade. Transparent governance and policies that support entrepreneurship help ensure that the benefits of wealth creation are distributed widely across society.

Shifting from Survival to Thriving

The move from poverty alleviation to wealth creation marks a shift in mindset—from surviving to thriving. In survival economies, scarcity defines behavior. People are consumed with meeting immediate needs and have little capacity to plan for the future. Wealth creation economies, on the other hand, are built on the principle of abundance—focusing on potential, opportunity, and growth.

This shift begins with rethinking how individuals and societies view their challenges. In wealth creation economies, people are encouraged to see limitations as opportunities and failures as stepping stones. A culture that celebrates innovation, resilience, and risk-taking must replace one that stigmatizes failure and discourages change.

Fostering this new mindset means creating environments where people are empowered to try, to fail, to learn, and to ultimately succeed. Such cultures reward initiative and create the foundation for innovation-driven progress.

Conclusion: A New Path Forward

Transitioning from poverty alleviation to wealth creation is not just about introducing new policies—it requires a deeper transformation in how Africans view themselves and their role in the global economy. Wealth creation is a generational process. It demands investment in people, in ideas, and in systems that promote innovation, entrepreneurship, and inclusive growth.

Africa's future should not be defined by survival but by flourishing—where every citizen can meet their basic needs and build lasting prosperity. By investing in education, improving access to capital, and encouraging bold thinking, African nations can break the cycle of dependency and usher in a new era of independence and economic resilience.

Aspirational Thinking for a Higher Version of Africa

Aspirational thinking challenges us to envision Africa not as it is, but as it could be—a continent where potential is fulfilled, barriers are overcome, and communities thrive in alignment with a shared vision. Embracing this mindset means moving beyond narratives rooted in limitation and instead focusing on possibility. It requires imagining a future defined by innovation, equity, and sustainable prosperity.

This shift in perspective encourages Africans to reframe the story of the continent—not through the lens of struggle, but through the power of resilience, creativity, and unity. Within this aspirational framework, growth is not limited to GDP or industrial output. It encompasses cultural, intellectual, and environmental progress, emphasizing a holistic model of development that

Generational Shift

honors Africa's heritage while propelling it toward a bold and transformative future.

To realize this higher version of Africa, leaders, educators, entrepreneurs, and everyday citizens must nurture a mindset of bold possibility. This means investing in spaces—both physical and ideological—where young Africans are encouraged to think ambitiously and creatively. Access to quality education, mentorship, and resources must be prioritized to cultivate critical thinking, innovation, and a culture of self-belief.

Policies that promote African languages, arts, and heritage can further reinforce a strong sense of identity and pride, anchoring progress in cultural richness. Meanwhile, engaging with the global community as equals—not dependents—can reposition Africa as a leading voice in global innovation, sustainability, and thought leadership.

Ultimately, aspirational thinking is the first step in building a continent that leads—not only in terms of economic power, but in vision, values, and human development. It is how Africa can inspire itself and the world—by dreaming boldly,

Chapter 15

acting decisively, and becoming a beacon of what's possible.

Chapter 16:
Africa's New Fight: From Dependency to Global Leadership

Africa's fight for colonial freedom remains one of the most defining movements in modern history. It marked the dawn of a new era—a moment when the aspirations for liberation, self-determination, and sovereignty began to take root. After centuries of exploitation, subjugation, and disenfranchisement under colonial rule, African nations started to emerge from the grip of European domination in the mid-20th century. This chapter revisits that monumental struggle for independence and argues that today's generation must carry the torch in a new fight—one that goes beyond political freedom to secure economic independence, shared prosperity, and continental leadership on the global stage.

Chapter 16

The Historical Fight for Colonial Freedom

Africa's colonial period formally began in the late 19th century following the Berlin Conference of 1884–1885, where European powers convened to divide the continent among themselves. This so-called "Scramble for Africa" saw colonial powers such as Britain, France, Belgium, Portugal, and Germany carve out territories for the purpose of resource extraction—stripping the continent of its raw materials, labor, and autonomy. Colonialism dismantled traditional systems of governance, imposed foreign political structures, and left behind a legacy of structural economic imbalance.

Among the most devastating consequences of colonial domination was the transatlantic slave trade. Over centuries, millions of Africans were forcibly taken from their homelands and subjected to unimaginable suffering. Their labor was exploited to build the wealth of empires abroad, while their societies were shattered at home. This system of forced extraction not only dehumanized an entire continent but also established the

Generational Shift

foundations of systemic inequality that persist to this day. The legacy of the slave trade is deeply embedded in Africa's socioeconomic fabric and underscores the need for a united push to dismantle lingering structures of external control.

Yet Africa's resistance never ceased. Throughout the colonial era, African societies pushed back—through armed uprisings, passive resistance, and intellectual advocacy. By the early 20th century, leaders such as Kwame Nkrumah of Ghana, Jomo Kenyatta of Kenya, Julius Nyerere of Tanzania, and Patrice Lumumba of the Congo emerged as visionaries for African liberation. Their fight extended beyond mere independence—they envisioned a united, self-sufficient Africa capable of charting its own path.

The movement gained momentum after World War II, as global anti-colonial sentiment intensified and European powers—exhausted from the war—could no longer maintain control. Ghana's independence in 1957 marked the beginning of a sweeping decolonization wave. Over the following decades, countries such as

Chapter 16

Nigeria (1960), Algeria (1962), and Kenya (1963) would follow, securing freedom through negotiations, mass mobilizations, and in many cases, long and painful armed struggles.

One of the most powerful symbols of the liberation era was Nelson Mandela, who devoted his life to ending apartheid in South Africa. His years of imprisonment and enduring commitment to peace and justice made him an emblem of resilience. Mandela's leadership inspired not only South Africa's transformation but also the broader African vision for dignity, unity, and self-determination.

While political independence was achieved, the post-colonial period introduced a new set of challenges. Many African states inherited fragile institutions, artificially drawn borders, and underdeveloped economies. The lack of economic infrastructure and administrative capacity, coupled with divisions rooted in colonial strategies, made nation-building a complex task.

Moreover, external control persisted in more subtle ways. Former colonial powers and new global actors continued to exert influence through multinational corporations, trade dependencies, foreign aid, and structural adjustment programs. These neo-colonial mechanisms restricted true sovereignty and locked many African nations into cycles of debt, dependency, and underdevelopment.

The first wave of liberation was about reclaiming political agency. The new wave must be about building economic autonomy, generating wealth from within, and establishing Africa as a global force—not one defined by need or dependency, but by value, innovation, and leadership.

The New Fight for African Advancement and True Freedom

Today's generation of Africans stands at the threshold of a new kind of struggle—not for liberation from colonial rulers, but for genuine self-reliance, prosperity, and global leadership. The mission now is to break the lingering cycle of dependency and redefine Africa's role in the world

Chapter 16

as a continent that commands its own future. This new fight rests on four critical pillars: advancement, prosperity, self-reliance, and strategic interdependence within the global economy.

1. African Advancement through Education and Innovation

The first step in reclaiming Africa's future is building intellectual and technological capacity. Quality education is the foundation for sustainable progress. Africa must now prioritize educational systems that prepare young people not just for employment—but for leadership in innovation, problem-solving, and entrepreneurship.

Too often, African education systems still reflect outdated colonial models that served the interests of foreign powers. These systems must be reimagined to reflect African priorities and potential. A stronger emphasis on STEM (science, technology, engineering, and mathematics), digital literacy, and vocational training will prepare the next generation to participate in—and shape—the digital economy and the future of work.

Equally important is fostering entrepreneurial thinking. Education should encourage African youth to become creators of opportunity, not just seekers of jobs. That means integrating business and innovation training into schools, universities, and community programs.

Africa is already proving it can lead in innovation. Kenya's M-Pesa mobile banking platform has revolutionized financial access across the continent, bypassing traditional banking systems to serve millions. Initiatives like this prove that Africa can leapfrog outdated technologies and deliver solutions tailored to its own needs. The future of African advancement lies in scaling these innovations, investing in local talent, and nurturing ecosystems that support entrepreneurship and creativity.

Chapter 16

2. Prosperity through Economic Independence and Wealth Creation

Africa's development narrative must shift from poverty reduction to wealth creation. Prosperity is not the absence of hardship; it is the presence of opportunity. Africa is rich in natural resources, human capital, and entrepreneurial spirit—but to harness this potential, nations must move up the value chain.

> "Today's generation must now carry the torch in a new fight – one that goes beyond political freedom and aims for economic independence, prosperity, and global leadership."

Exporting raw materials while importing finished products continues to drain value and jobs from African economies. Economic independence begins with value addition—investing in processing, manufacturing, and homegrown industries that build capacity and create employment. This requires a commitment to infrastructure—especially in power, transport, and digital access—as well as policies that foster innovation and industrialization.

The African Continental Free Trade Area (AfCFTA) is a landmark opportunity. By boosting intra-African trade, AfCFTA can reduce external dependency and stimulate local production, allowing African nations to sell to each other, build stronger supply chains, and retain wealth within the continent. A unified African market is key to strengthening resilience and unlocking shared prosperity.

3. Self-Reliance: Reducing Aid Dependency

Decades after political independence, too many African countries remain economically dependent on foreign aid. While humanitarian assistance has played a role in times of crisis, sustained reliance on aid has stunted self-reliance, weakened accountability, and allowed external interests to shape domestic priorities.

True independence requires a shift—from external support to internal strength. That means mobilizing domestic resources: improving tax

Chapter 16

> "Africa's vast natural resources, youthful population, and growing middle class present immense opportunities for economic growth, but these must be harnessed through sustainable strategies that focus on value addition, industrialization, and trade."

systems, managing natural resources effectively, and promoting policies that stimulate entrepreneurship and private sector growth. African governments must commit to efficient, transparent governance that channels national wealth into national development.

Foreign direct investment (FDI) must also be viewed through a long-term lens. The goal is not just to attract capital—but to ensure that investments build local capacity, transfer skills, and create sustainable impact rather than extract resources.

Perhaps most importantly, self-reliance starts with a mindset. Africans must believe in their own capacity to solve problems, create solutions, and lead progress. Rwanda's Vision 2020 program is a case in point. By emphasizing good governance, private-sector growth, and homegrown solutions, Rwanda has transformed itself into one of Africa's fastest-growing economies. Its model demonstrates that self-reliance is not a dream—it is an achievable strategy.

4. Global Interdependence: Africa as an Equal Player on the World Stage

As Africa advances toward self-reliance and prosperity, the goal is not isolation but meaningful integration within the global community. True independence means engaging with the world on equal footing—shaping global narratives, influencing policy, and participating in partnerships that are based on equity and mutual benefit.

To do this, Africa must redefine its role in international trade. It can no longer afford to be seen solely as a source of raw materials; it must position itself as a producer of high-value goods and services. This shift will require bold

Chapter 16

leadership, regional collaboration, and a unified voice in global trade negotiations. African leaders and institutions must advocate for fair trade practices, equitable market access, and an end to exploitative trade terms that disadvantage the continent.

Beyond economics, Africa's contributions to global culture, knowledge, and innovation must be championed. African music, art, literature, and fashion already captivate audiences worldwide. Its thought leadership on issues like climate resilience, youth development, and social justice offers fresh perspectives urgently needed on the global stage. By asserting these contributions with confidence, Africa not only claims its rightful place in global discourse but also shapes the future of that discourse.

Interdependence means that Africa does not seek separation from the world, but respect within it—contributing ideas, solutions, and value on its own terms.

Conclusion: The Path to Global Leadership

The new fight for Africa is not about retreating from the world—it is about rising within it. It is about completing the unfinished work of liberation: not just claiming political independence, but achieving economic sovereignty, social equity, and global influence.

Africa's future lies not in handouts or foreign prescriptions, but in the ingenuity, resilience, and determination of its people. Today's generation must lead the way—harnessing the continent's wealth of natural resources, human capital, and cultural legacy to build an Africa that is confident, self-reliant, and globally engaged.

The battles of past generations delivered political freedom. The task now is to secure dignity, prosperity, and leadership. Africa must become a global force not by imitating others but by elevating its own voice, its own values, and its own vision.

Chapter 16

This is Africa's moment—an opportunity to lead, to inspire, and to transform not just the continent, but the world. The responsibility falls to this generation: to dream boldly, act decisively, and shape a future where Africa stands not in the shadows of others, but at the forefront of global progress.

Chapter 17:
The Role of Africa's Diaspora in Advancing Progress

Africa's diaspora holds immense potential to drive the continent's transformation. With more than 140 million Africans living abroad—representing roughly 10 percent of Africa's global family—the diaspora embodies a powerful blend of cultural connection, global experience, and diverse skill sets. Across sectors such as healthcare, education, entrepreneurship, technology, and infrastructure, the diaspora is uniquely positioned to contribute to Africa's development in meaningful and lasting ways.

From remittances and investments to knowledge transfer, mentorship, and advocacy, diaspora engagement is no longer a peripheral consideration—it is a central pillar in the journey toward African prosperity, sustainability, and independence. However, diaspora involvement must be rooted in more than financial support. It

Chapter 17

must reflect a mutually beneficial partnership—grounded in shared vision, collective responsibility, and a deep commitment to building a thriving, dignified, and unified Africa. An Africa that every African—at home or abroad—can be proud of.

Pathways for Diaspora Engagement

There are numerous ways in which members of the African diaspora can contribute to the continent's advancement, depending on their resources, expertise, and passions. These contributions extend far beyond family remittances and can serve as catalysts for systemic change.

1. Financial Investments and Remittances

Diaspora remittances remain a vital source of income for millions across the continent. In 2022 alone, sub-Saharan Africa received over $53 billion in remittances, bolstering household incomes and helping to cover essentials like education, healthcare, and small business operations. But the potential goes even further.

Beyond basic remittances, targeted investments from the diaspora can stimulate economic growth and support emerging sectors. By investing in local startups, SMEs, real estate, and infrastructure projects, diaspora members can help generate employment, increase local productivity, and spur innovation. Countries like Ethiopia have already introduced **diaspora bonds**, enabling Africans abroad to invest directly in national development initiatives—funding roads, energy, and housing projects critical to long-term progress.

2. **Knowledge Transfer and Skills Development**

Africa's diaspora community includes thousands of highly skilled professionals across key fields—technology, medicine, finance, education, law, and engineering, among others. Tapping into this vast talent pool offers an invaluable opportunity for skills transfer and institutional development.

Programs such as Kenya's **Brain Gain Initiative** or Rwanda's targeted recruitment of skilled diaspora professionals encourage temporary or permanent return of expertise. These initiatives allow diaspora members to mentor, train, teach, and collaborate with local institutions, bridging gaps in technical knowledge and supporting capacity-building. Whether through guest lecturing, virtual mentorships, or project collaborations, knowledge exchange can be a cornerstone of self-sustaining development on the continent.

3. Philanthropy and Social Entrepreneurship

Many in the diaspora are actively involved in philanthropic projects focused on education, public health, and social services. These efforts range from funding school construction and scholarships to sponsoring mobile clinics and clean water initiatives. When paired with innovation, philanthropy becomes even more powerful.

Social entrepreneurship—which blends business goals with social impact—is gaining momentum among diaspora communities. Take the example of Ugandan-American entrepreneur **Patrick Awuah**, who founded Ashesi University in

Ghana to promote ethical leadership and high-quality education. Such initiatives do more than address immediate needs; they empower local communities, build institutions, and create lasting impact at scale.

4. Advocacy and Policy Influence

Diaspora communities also play a critical role in amplifying Africa's voice on the global stage. Through civic engagement and political organizing, diaspora groups can advocate for equitable policies on trade, immigration, education, public health, and international development.

For instance, the passage of the **African Growth and Opportunity Act (AGOA)** — which improves market access for African exports to the U.S. — was influenced in part by organized diaspora advocacy. Similar efforts can strengthen Africa's global presence, promote fair partnerships, and support representation in global institutions.

Chapter 17

As Africa's population rapidly expands—it is projected to reach nearly **3 billion by 2050**—the role of its diaspora in shaping equitable international relations will become even more critical. With the continent home to one of the youngest populations on Earth, the time is now to leverage global partnerships and diaspora networks to shape a stronger, more unified African future.

Africa's diaspora is not separate from the continent—it is an extension of it. Its members carry with them a deep reservoir of knowledge, networks, experience, and capital that can meaningfully contribute to Africa's rise.

By forging new paths of engagement—from investment and mentorship to advocacy and innovation—the diaspora can help build an Africa that is not defined by need, but by vision. A continent that does not look outward for validation but inward for leadership. This reimagined partnership calls for intentional collaboration rooted in pride, purpose, and shared responsibility.

Africa's progress will not be complete without its diaspora. And the diaspora's influence will not reach its fullest potential until it reconnects with the land, the people, and the vision that binds us all.

Examples of Diaspora Contributions to Development in LMICs

Around the world, low- and middle-income countries (LMICs) have benefited significantly from the engagement of their diaspora communities. These examples offer valuable insights into how the African diaspora can play a similarly transformative role in advancing development on the continent:

1. India

The Indian diaspora—one of the world's largest and most economically influential—has played a pivotal role in India's emergence as a global tech leader. Through investments in education and technology, Indian expatriates have helped establish innovation hubs in cities like Bengaluru and Hyderabad. Organizations such as **TiE (The**

Chapter 17

Indus Entrepreneurs) were launched to mentor Indian entrepreneurs, connect them with global networks, and provide capital. India's booming tech sector demonstrates the power of diaspora-led initiatives in advancing economic transformation.

2. China

China's economic rise has been significantly supported by its global diaspora, particularly Chinese communities in Southeast Asia and the West. During the country's reform era in the late 20th century, Chinese diaspora investors helped fund industrial zones and manufacturing centers.

> "The involvement of the diaspora is essential for accelerating progress across sectors such as healthcare, education, entrepreneurship, and infrastructure. By reconnecting with Africa's development, the diaspora can help address challenges while creating opportunities that lead to sustained growth, prosperity, and independence."

This early wave of investment laid the groundwork for China's industrialization. The Chinese government actively facilitated this involvement through targeted policies and incentives—offering a blueprint for how African nations can encourage productive diaspora investment.

3. Ethiopia

Ethiopia has successfully engaged its diaspora through initiatives like the **diaspora bond**, used to fund major projects such as the **Grand Ethiopian Renaissance Dam**. This approach enabled Ethiopians abroad to invest directly in national development and share ownership in a transformative infrastructure project. Ethiopia's model shows how national pride and a clear development vision can mobilize diaspora resources for the public good.

4. Jamaica

Jamaica's diaspora has contributed meaningfully across education, tourism, and healthcare. The government's **Global Jamaica Diaspora Council**

Chapter 17

fosters engagement through initiatives like medical missions, investment in infrastructure, and business development programs. By actively incorporating diaspora voices into national development, Jamaica has attracted both capital and expertise from its global community.

Creating Welcoming Spaces for Diaspora Involvement in Africa

For Africa to fully harness the power of its diaspora, governments and communities must create inclusive, enabling environments that recognize diaspora members as collaborators—not just donors or outsiders. This shift requires proactive policies, grassroots engagement, and a renewed cultural narrative around partnership and unity.

1. Policy Support and Incentives

Governments can support diaspora engagement by implementing policies that reduce barriers to investment and participation. These may include tax incentives, simplified business registration processes, dual citizenship options, and dedicated diaspora liaison offices within foreign missions.

A notable example is Ghana's **"Year of Return"** campaign, which invited Africans abroad to reconnect with their heritage and invest in the country—resulting in millions of dollars in economic contributions and renewed cultural ties. Institutional frameworks that make diaspora participation accessible and rewarding are essential for long-term engagement.

2. Community Engagement and Collaboration

Beyond policy, community-level engagement is key. Diaspora members should be seen as collaborators in progress, not external benefactors. Programs that encourage dialogue and shared initiatives between local residents and diaspora professionals—such as cultural exchanges, joint ventures, and co-hosted development projects—can foster mutual understanding and trust.

This collaboration must be grounded in mutual respect: communities must recognize the resources and experience the diaspora brings,

Chapter 17

while diaspora members must honor the knowledge and resilience of local stakeholders.

3. Building a Culture of Respect and Partnership

Transformative change happens when development is approached as a **shared mission**. Africa's future will be most powerfully shaped when its global citizens—both at home and abroad—work together in a spirit of co-creation. A culture of respect and partnership must be cultivated, where diasporans are not romanticized or resented, but embraced as an extension of the continent's family with shared responsibility.

True partnership means honoring local leadership while embracing diaspora skills and networks as complementary assets. When approached in this way, diaspora engagement becomes a powerful force for both individual and collective empowerment.

Conclusion: Embracing the Diaspora as Partners in Africa's Growth

The African diaspora holds untapped potential to shape the continent's development narrative—not only through capital or skills, but through advocacy, leadership, and global influence. When aligned with the needs of local communities and supported by thoughtful policy, diaspora engagement can become a cornerstone of Africa's transformation.

This chapter calls on both continental and diaspora Africans to recognize their **shared future**. The challenges Africa faces are not confined by borders—and neither are the solutions. By fostering inclusive systems, championing unity, and encouraging purposeful collaboration, Africa can move toward a future of prosperity, dignity, and interdependence—powered by the full strength of its global family.

Africa's story is still being written. And its diaspora must be among the authors of the next chapter.

Chapter 18:
Chasing the African Dream

The African Dream is more than an abstract ideal – it is a tangible, transformative vision of what Africa can become. To chase this dream is to pursue a future where our societies are rooted in decency, honesty, integrity, and strong family values. It is about building communities where people feel safe, respected, and empowered to thrive. The African Dream is not out of reach. It is possible – if we are willing to bring out our better angels and leave behind the destructive patterns of the past.

> Are we ready to dream for Africa as much as we dream for the West?

Building a Desirable Society

A desirable society begins with recognizing our shared humanity. It is one where kindness and decency are not exceptions but norms – where honesty and integrity guide both citizens and leaders. When leaders exemplify these values, they inspire trust and create the foundation for a society in which people can flourish. Corruption, dishonesty, and self-interest have weakened the social fabric of too many African nations. To pursue the African Dream, we must commit to repairing that fabric with transparency, accountability, and trust.

Strong families form the foundation of a strong society. They are where values are passed down, identities are shaped, and futures are built. Societies that invest in the well-being of families – through education, healthcare, and opportunity – build a generation equipped to lead, innovate, and contribute. By strengthening our families, we strengthen our communities, and in doing so, strengthen our nations.

Rejecting Violence and Embracing Peace

Violence has never solved Africa's deepest challenges. From civil wars to ethnic conflicts, the damage caused by violence is enduring – leaving behind fear, poverty, and instability. The African

Chapter 18

Dream demands that we reject violence in all its forms and instead embrace dialogue, reconciliation, and unity.

Bringing out our better angels means choosing peace over power, understanding over hatred, and unity over division. It means recognizing that we are not enemies but partners in building something greater. A peaceful society is fertile ground for creativity, entrepreneurship, and cooperation – the cornerstones of lasting development.

Strengthening Communities

The African Dream is not an individual pursuit. It is a collective journey. Every African has a role to play in strengthening their community – whether through civic engagement, mentorship,

> To chase the African Dream is to pursue a future where our societies are built on the foundation of basic human decency, honesty, integrity, and strong family values.

entrepreneurship, or simply by being a responsible citizen.

Communities grow stronger when individuals invest in one another – by supporting local businesses, participating in community initiatives, and championing policies that promote equity and inclusion. When we take collective ownership of local challenges, we build resilience – communities that not only survive adversity but rise above it.

Why the African Dream?

Why is it that so many Africans chase the American Dream, while the African Dream remains overlooked? Why do thousands risk their lives for opportunities abroad when our own continent holds so much untapped potential?

The appeal of the American Dream lies in its promise of opportunity, prosperity, and freedom. But shouldn't those same promises be available here – in our own homelands? The African Dream is not about imitating other societies. It is about building a future that reflects our values, heritage, and vision. It is about reclaiming the narrative and defining success on our terms.

If we direct the same ambition, energy, and determination toward our communities as we do chasing opportunities abroad, imagine what Africa could look like in 10, 20, or 50 years. We have the resources, talent, and resilience needed to make this dream real. The only question is: Are we ready to dream for Africa as boldly as we dream for the West?

A Vision for a Secure and Prosperous Future

The African Dream envisions a continent where families can live without fear, where opportunities abound, and where every individual can realize their full potential. It is a vision rooted in **security** – not just physical safety, but economic and social security as well.

That security comes from systems that work, institutions that protect, and opportunities that uplift. It means living in societies where the rule of law is respected, fairness is upheld, and no one is left behind. If we are to make Africa a place where families thrive and wealth is built across generations, we must address the root causes of insecurity and build inclusive systems that truly serve the people.

The Call to Action

Chasing the African Dream is a call to action – for Africans on the continent and across the diaspora. It is a call to rise beyond the limitations of the past and embrace the possibilities of the future. It is a call to build societies defined not by what we have endured, but by what we envision.

Let us commit to the values of decency, honesty, and integrity. Let us fortify our families and uplift our communities. Let us reject the cycles of violence and build cultures of peace. Let us collaborate – across borders, generations, and sectors – to create an Africa that is not only desirable, but exemplary.

The African Dream is not a fantasy. It is a promise – and with unity, purpose, and belief in

Chapter 18

our collective strength, it is a promise we can fulfill.

Chapter 19:
A Vision for Africa's Future – Pathways to True Independence and Prosperity

As we conclude this journey through the ideas and principles explored in *Generational Shift: Shift Mindsets, Break Cycles, and Embrace New Ideas for Africa's Growth*, a powerful vision for Africa's future comes into focus – one where the continent achieves true independence, sustainability, and

> The vision for Africa's growth rests on rejecting the cycles of dependency and embracing solutions driven by Africans, for Africans, rooted in the continent's rich heritage and forward-thinking dynamism.

global relevance by drawing strength from within.

Throughout this book, we have examined recurring themes such as brain drain, capital escape, youth empowerment, women's

Chapter 19

leadership, innovation, and environmental stewardship. These threads are all interconnected, pointing to the urgent need for a generational shift in mindset – one that discards dependency and embraces African-driven solutions, rooted in the continent's rich heritage and future-forward dynamism.

This transformation begins with perspective. By fostering opportunity economies, promoting critical thinking through education, and cultivating a culture of innovation and inclusive governance, Africa can chart a new course. A course where the next generation is no longer defined by inherited challenges but inspired by bold aspirations. Africa's diversity – its people, resources, cultures, and ideas – is its greatest strength.

> **Africa's future will be shaped by those who dare to break the cycle, who engage in aspirational thinking, and who commit to building an Africa that is both self-sufficient and globally influential.**

Generational Shift

The youth stand at the center of this shift. Africa's future will be defined by those who choose to lead, disrupt harmful norms, and create new systems that reflect integrity, opportunity, and inclusion. It is their responsibility to fight not colonial powers, but outdated traditions, corrupt systems, and limiting beliefs that no longer serve the continent.

Africa's moment is now – and its greatest asset is its people.

Africa's Greatest Foe: Confronting the Enemy Within

Africa's victories over colonial powers were historic milestones, marking a powerful reclamation of sovereignty. But decades after independence, the most persistent threats are no longer external – they are internal. Corruption, tribalism, weak institutions, and a lack of accountability continue to stifle Africa's growth.

True independence will only be realized when African nations confront these internal obstacles head-on. This means dismantling self-

Chapter 19

imposed cycles of underdevelopment and embracing collective responsibility. Leaders must govern with integrity. Citizens must hold them accountable. Institutions must serve the people.

The work ahead is as critical as the struggles of past generations. This is a call for introspection, bold leadership, and visionary action. The future is not promised – it must be built. The ideas in this book serve as a roadmap for those ready to take up the challenge and redefine what it means to live, build, and thrive in Africa.

The task is ours. The time is now.

Discussion Questions

The following questions are designed to encourage critical reflection and conversation around the key themes of *Generational Shift*. They can be used in book clubs, classrooms, community forums, or leadership circles to inspire practical solutions for Africa's growth.

Entrepreneurship and Innovation

1. **Unlocking Potential through Entrepreneurship**

    - Africa is rich in both human and natural resources, yet much of its potential remains untapped. Which sectors offer the greatest opportunities for entrepreneurial growth?

    - What support systems – such as mentorship, capital access, or policy reforms – are essential for young African entrepreneurs to thrive?

2. **Innovation for Local Challenges**

    - What are some examples of African innovations that have successfully addressed local needs?

    - How can we ensure these solutions are scalable, sustainable, and transferable across diverse regions of the continent?

3. **Overcoming Barriers to Entrepreneurship**

    - Entrepreneurs across Africa often face similar challenges: limited funding, infrastructure gaps, and lack of mentorship. What policies or programs could help break down these barriers?

4. **Technology and Digital Transformation**

   - How can African countries better harness digital tools to drive development and close the digital divide?

   - What role should governments and private sectors play in expanding digital literacy and internet access?

5. **Social Entrepreneurship**

   - How can businesses balance profit with purpose to address critical social challenges?

   - What issues in your own community could be addressed through social entrepreneurship, and what would it take to get started?

Governance and Ethical Leadership

1. Ethical Leadership for Africa's Future

The book emphasizes the importance of integrity and justice in leadership.

- What qualities define an ethical African leader in today's context?
- How can these values be instilled and reinforced in current and future generations?

2. Combating Corruption

Corruption remains one of the most significant barriers to Africa's development.

- What practical steps can governments, citizens, and civil society organizations take to promote transparency, accountability, and good governance?

3. Youth Engagement in Governance

Young people form the majority of Africa's population.

Chapter 19

- How can they be meaningfully involved in governance and decision-making?
- What policies or structures can ensure their voices are not only heard but also implemented?

4. Tribalism and Inclusive Governance

Tribalism and nepotism continue to influence politics across the continent.

- What can be done to promote national unity and ensure inclusive governance that transcends ethnic lines?

5. Justice and Righteousness in Leadership

Drawing from the chapter on biblical values:

- How can the principles of righteousness and justice be applied in African governance today?
- Are there African leaders or policies that exemplify these values?

New Ideas and Vision for Africa's Growth

1. From Poverty Reduction to Wealth Creation

The book calls for a mindset shift from survival to prosperity.

- What does wealth creation look like in the African context?
- How can communities and individuals move beyond aid-based models to create lasting prosperity?

2. Diaspora Engagement

Africa's global diaspora holds great potential for development.

- How can countries better engage the diaspora for investments, mentorship, and policy advocacy?
- What programs or incentives might strengthen this partnership?

3. Generational Shift

Change often comes through bold new thinking.

Chapter 19

- What role does the next generation play in challenging old systems and adopting new ideas?
- How can young Africans lead the charge in redefining governance, entrepreneurship, and social values?

4. Opportunity Economies

The concept of opportunity economies is central to this book.

- How can African nations create systems that provide equitable access to education, capital, and innovation?
- What policies or investments are essential to ensure that no one is left behind?

5. Vision for Africa's Future

Looking ahead 30 years:

- What does a prosperous, independent, and globally respected Africa look like?
- What specific steps can be taken today to lay the foundation for that future?

Call to Action

1. Personal Responsibility

Every African has a role to play in the continent's transformation.

- What are practical ways individuals can contribute through entrepreneurship, community service, advocacy, or leadership?
- What steps can you take to foster progress in your own sphere of influence?

2. Collaborative Efforts

Progress requires unity and collaboration.

- How can African countries work together to create a unified, cohesive vision for development?
- What roles do regional institutions like the African Union and AfCFTA play in building this collective future?

3. Sustaining Momentum

True transformation is a long-term effort.

Chapter 19

- How can Africa's youth, leaders, and diaspora stay committed to the vision laid out in this book?
- What systems or habits can help sustain change across generations?

These discussion questions are designed to provoke deep reflection and practical dialogue. Whether in classrooms, community groups, leadership forums, or private study, they serve as a tool to translate insight into action – helping readers become catalysts in Africa's generational shift.

References

Acemoglu, D., & Robinson, J. A. (2012). *Why Nations Fail: The Origins of Power, Prosperity, and Poverty.* Crown Publishing Group.

African Development Bank. (2021). *African Economic Outlook 2021: From Debt Resolution to Growth: The Road Ahead for Africa.* Retrieved from www.afdb.org.

Collier, P. (2007). *The Bottom Billion: Why the Poorest Countries Are Failing and What Can Be Done About It.* Oxford University Press.

Easterly, W. (2006). *The White Man's Burden: Why the West's Efforts to Aid the Rest Have Done So Much Ill and So Little Good.* Penguin Press.

Gates, B. (2019). *How to Avoid a Climate Disaster: The Solutions We Have and the Breakthroughs We Need.* Knopf Publishing.

Moyo, D. (2009). *Dead Aid: Why Aid Is Not Working and How There Is a Better Way for Africa.* Farrar, Straus, and Giroux.

Ndulu, B., Chakraborti, L., Lijane, L., Ramachandran, V., & Wolgin, J. (2007). *Challenges of African Growth: Opportunities, Constraints, and Strategic Directions.* The World Bank.

Rodrik, D. (2017). *Straight Talk on Trade: Ideas for a Sane World Economy.* Princeton University Press.

Sachs, J. D. (2005). *The End of Poverty: Economic Possibilities for Our Time.* Penguin Press.

United Nations Economic Commission for Africa (UNECA). (2020). *The Role of the African Continental Free Trade Area (AfCFTA) in Post-COVID-19 Africa.* Retrieved from www.uneca.org.

World Bank. (2022). *Africa's Pulse: An Analysis of Issues Shaping Africa's Economic Future.*

Retrieved from www.worldbank.org.

www.ingramcontent.com/pod-product-compliance
Lightning Source LLC
Chambersburg PA
CBHW060455030426
42337CB00015B/1603